Business to Business

Englische Geschäftskorrespondenz und Bürokommunikation

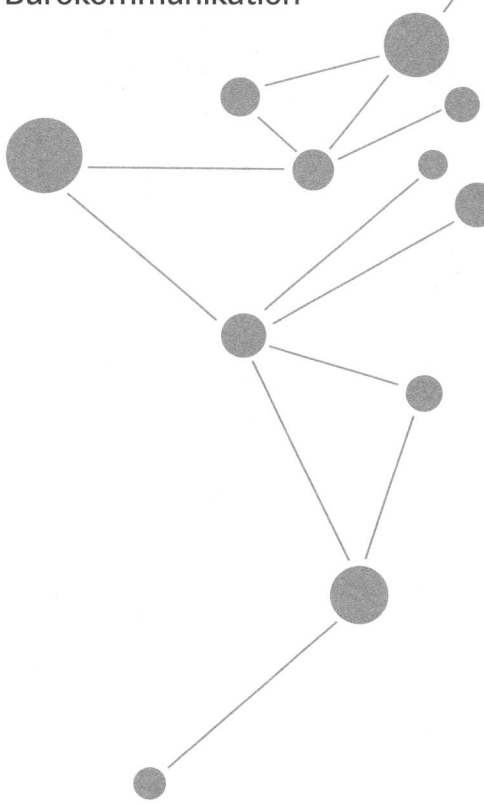

Praxishandbuch

von
Ruth Feiertag
Dr. Richard Hooton
Ulrich Boltz

Ernst Klett Verlag
Stuttgart · Leipzig

Business to Business
Englische Geschäftskorrespondenz und Bürokommunikation
Praxishandbuch

Autoren: Ruth Feiertag, Dr. Richard Hooton, Ulrich Boltz

Werkübersicht:

Schülerbuch, 978-3-12-808247-9
Lehrerhandbuch, inkl. Digitalem Lehrer-Service und 2 Audio-CDs, 978-3-12-808251-6
Workbook, inkl. Audio-CD-ROM und IHK Prüfungsvorbereitung, 978-3-12-808249-3
Praxishandbuch, 978-3-12-808250-9

1. Auflage | 5 4 3 2 1 |
1 | 19 18 17 16 15

Redaktion: Volker Wendland
Herstellung: Sarah Ganser

Satz: typoschneiderei, Wien
Gestaltung: kognito gestaltung, Berlin
Reproduktion: Meyle + Müller Medien-Management, Pforzheim
Druck: Himmer AG, Augsburg
Presswerk: Osswald GmbH & Co., Leinfelden-Echterdingen

Printed in Germany
ISBN 978-3-12-808250-9

Inhaltsverzeichnis

1 Introductions   5

A | Introduction   5
B | Model introduction of a company   6
C | Tool kit   6
1 Phrases: Introducing yourself and others   6
2 Phrases: Introducing a business, describing its products/services   7
D | Avoiding common mistakes   7

2 Layout of business letters and e-mails   8

A | Introduction   8
B | Model letters and e-mails   9
1 Model letter   9
2 Model e-mail   10
C | Tool kit   10
1 Elements of business letters   10
2 Elements of e-mails   13
3 Useful tips: Old-fashioned and modern   14

3 Telephoning   15

A | Introduction   15
B | Model dialogue   16
C | Tool kit   18
1 Telephone alphabet   18
2 Punctuation   18
3 Dictation   19
4 Useful telephone phrases   20
5 Typical phrases (German/English): Telephoning   22

4 Making arrangements   23

A | Introduction   23
B | Model e-mails and model telephone dialogue   24
1 Invitations   24
2 Bookings   26
C | Tool kit   27
1 Useful phrases for welcoming a visitor   27
2 Building blocks: Secretarial communication   28
3 Building blocks: Fairs and exhibitions   29
4 Typical phrases (German/English): Making arrangements   30

5 Enquiries   31

A | Introduction   31
B | Model enquiries by e-mail and on the phone   32
1 Enquiry by e-mail/letter   32
2 Enquiry by telephone   33
C | Tool kit   34
1 Building blocks for business communications: Enquiries   34
2 Typical phrases (German/English): Enquiries   36
3 Structural elements of business correspondence   37
D | Avoiding common mistakes   37

6 Offers   38

A | Introduction   38
B | Model correspondence   39
1 Offer by letter   39
2 Offer by e-mail   40
3 Offer by phone   40
C | Tool kit   41
1 Building blocks for business communications: Replies to enquiries/Making offers   41
2 Typical phrases (German/English): Offers   44
D | Avoiding common mistakes   45

7 Comparing offers and presenting products and statistics   46

A | Introduction   46
B | Model offer and model product presentation   47
1 Offer   47
2 Product presentation   48
C | Tool kit   48
1 Phrases: Comparing products   48
2 Building blocks for business communications: Presentations   49
3 Describing graphs and diagrams   50
4 Typical phrases (German/English): Presentations   52

8 Orders   54

A | Introduction   54
1 Legal aspects   54
2 Commercial aspects   55
B | Model orders   56
1 Model letter and order form   56
2 Structure of a detailed order   57
C | Tool kit   57
1 Building blocks for business communications: Orders   57
2 Typical phrases: Orders   59
D | Avoiding common mistakes   60

9 Order confirmation and cancellation   61

A | Introduction   61
B | Model letters   62
1 Cancellation of order by letter   62
2 Order confirmation by e-mail   63
3 Informal confirmation by e-mail   63
C | Tool kit   64
1 Building blocks for business communications: Confirmation and cancellation of orders   64
2 An order form   66
D | Avoiding common mistakes   66

10 Payment · 67

A | Introduction · 67
B | Model fax · 71
C | Tool kit · 71
1 Building blocks for business communications: Payment · 71
2 Typical phrases (German/English): Payment · 73
D | Avoiding common mistakes · 74

11 Credit enquiries · 75

A | Introduction · 75
B | Model letters · 76
1 Structure of a detailed enquiry · 76
2 Credit enquiry · 77
3 Credit information · 78
C | Tool kit · 80
1 Building blocks for business communications:
Credit enquiries · 80
2 Typical phrases (German/English): Credit enquiries · 81
3 Building blocks for business communications:
Credit information · 82
4 Typical phrases (German/English): Credit information · 83
D | Avoiding common mistakes · 84

12 Delivery · 85

A | Introduction · 85
B | Model letter: Dispatch advice · 86
C | Tool kit · 87
1 Building blocks for business communications: Delivery · 87
2 Building blocks for business communications:
Dispatch advice · 87
3 Typical phrases (German/English): Delivery · 89
D | Avoiding common mistakes · 89

13 Complaints and adjustments · 90

A | Introduction · 90
B | Model e-mail: Apology and adjustment · 91
C | Tool kit · 92
1 Building blocks for business communications:
Complaints · 92
2 Typical phrases (German/English): Complaints · 94
3 Building blocks for business communications:
Replies to complaints · 95
4 Typical phrases (German/English): Adjustments · 97
D | Avoiding common mistakes · 98

14 Reminders · 99

A | Introduction · 99
B | Model letters and model telephone conversation · 100
1 Structure of a detailed reminder · 100
2 Structure of a detailed reply to a reminder · 101
3 Telephone conversation · 101
C | Tool kit · 102
1 Building blocks for business communications:
Reminders · 102

2 Typical phrases (German/English): Reminders · 104
3 Building blocks for business communications:
Replies to reminders · 104
4 Typical phrases (German/English): Replies to reminders · 107
D | Avoiding common mistakes · 108

15 Marketing and sales · 109

A | Introduction · 109
B | Model letters/ e-mail · 110
1 Enquiry about co-operation · 110
2 Informal marketing letter · 110
3 Offer to act as an agent · 112
C | Tool kit · 113
1 Building blocks for business communications: Agencies · 113
2 Typical phrases (German/English): Marketing and sales · 115
D | Avoiding common mistakes · 115

16 Job applications · 116

A | Introduction · 116
B | Model application letter, CV and job interview · 117
1 Application letter · 117
2 CV (German/English) · 118
3 Job interview · 120
C | Tool kit · 121
1 Phrases: Application · 121
2 Job titles (German/English) · 122

17 Socializing in a business environment · 123

A | Introduction · 123
B | Model dialogue/e-mail/letter · 124
1 Model dialogue: The company "do" and private events · 124
2 E-mail: Announcing an office get-together · 126
3 Letter: Written invitation · 126
4 Letter: Congratulations · 127
5 Letter: Condolence · 128
C | Tool kit · 128

Anhang · 130

1 Memos and reports · 130
2 Incoterms 2010 · 131
3 Sales contract · 133
4 Negotiations · 134
5 Cheques and banker's drafts · 135
6 Bills of exchange · 136
7 Types of firms and companies · 137
8 Organisation of companies · 139
9 Titles in British and US companies · 139
10 Types of packaging · 140
11 Handling marks · 140
12 Insurance · 141
13 Documents in foreign trade · 142
14 Organisations and associations · 144
15 Distribution channels · 146
Alphabetical word list · 148

Introductions

A | Introduction

In business life you often have to introduce yourself or your company. Especially in the case of companies it is important to be aware of the image you wish to project and of the extent to which you are
5 achieving this.

Since so much business is conducted online it is essential to have an attractive, well-designed and easy to use website, especially if online sales are an important part of your turnover. If it's difficult for
10 customers to find their way around the website or there's a frustrating amount of information they are not interested in, they soon give up and go elsewhere. The design of the website and also the design and layout of publications, letterhead and
15 business cards are part of the way in which companies introduce themselves and position themselves in the competition for customers. An imaginative, memorable and possibly witty logo, company name and motto, plus an arresting use of colour are all
20 ingredients in the presentation of the company.

When introducing themselves to the public companies have to decide what values to project – for instance, young and dynamic or traditional, solid and reliable. Are they, for instance, in the business
25 of offering products that cater for (and often create!) fantasies or functional products based on technical knowhow? Is it important for the company to be seen as caring or environment-friendly? These are important issues for all companies. Larger com-
30 panies have marketing and PR (Public Relations) departments whose role it is to provide information and help project a particular image. Nearly all companies have at least one person who is responsible for marketing and PR matters.

35 The employees of a company are also an important part of the way in which a company presents itself. Are they friendly? Do they make an efficient and businesslike impression? Do they signal: Customers are important – we take their well-being, require-
40 ments and complaints seriously?

B | Model introduction of a company

"My name is Pia Westhoff from *Strawberry Fair*.
Strawberry Fair is an important manufacturer of young fashion selling to many retail outlets focussed on this huge and economically very important segment throughout Europe and North America. Fashion for teenagers and twenty-somethings is a very fast moving and vibrant business. We produce affordable fashion for both sexes which incorporates designer ideas – we are constantly on the look-out for innovative and creative inspiration to ensure that we keep up with new trends and also add original features of our own. Originality is a top priority for people in our target group, which has considerable purchasing power. The sector is, of course, hugely competitive both in terms of creativity and prices. For this reason, we have many garments manufactured according to our designs and standards in countries where wages are lower than in Western Europe. As an ethically aware company we are also concerned to ensure that minimal social and safety standards are maintained.
We exhibit at many major fashion fairs in Europe and the US. Come and see our exciting new collections or request a list of outlets in your area featuring our garments."

C | Tool kit

1 Phrases: Introducing yourself and others

Hello, I'm Susan.

My name is Henry Crawford. Please call me Henry.

My surname is Jansen, my first name is Markus.

I'm from Berlin.

I am British/German/... .

I'm 22 years old.

I was born in Manchester on 7 June 1993.

I'm a trainee export clerk.

I'm training as an office management assistant.

I am Mrs Bennet's personal assistant.

I am interested in computer games.

I love travelling more than anything else.

I'm into kite-surfing.

Have you met Mr. Richardson? – Reply: Hello. Pleased/Nice to meet you.

May I introduce Dr. Martens?

How are you? How are you doing? – Reply: Fine./Not too bad.

2 Phrases: Introducing a business, describing its products/services

I'm … assistant sales manager at … .

My name is … , I'm in charge of purchasing office supplies.

We are a leading manufacturer of … .

We specialize in providing the following services: …

We are a wholesaler specializing in …

We are a chain of … retailers.

Our firm is a major provider of … .

We offer state-of-the-art solutions for … .

We make a wide range of high-quality … .

Our … are in high demand all over the world.

We import … from … .

Our … are both reliable and long-lasting.

The excellent … we offer will appeal to your discerning customers.

D | Avoiding common mistakes

Wrong	Correct
1. I'm ~~of~~ Hamburg.	1. I'm **from** Hamburg.
2. I ~~am~~ born in Dresden.	2. I **was** born in Dresden.
3. I was born ~~at~~ 29 December 1994	3. I was born **on** 29 December 1994.
4. I was born ~~on 7 June 1994 in Dresden~~.	4. I was born **in Dresden on 7 June 1994**.
5. I'm training ~~as event~~ manager.	5. I'm training **as an event** manager.
6. She works ~~as personal~~ assistant.	6. She works **as a personal** assistant.
7. I ~~am computer~~ programmer.	7. I **am a computer** programmer.
8. We ~~are specialized~~ in manufacturing …	8. We **specialize** in manufacturing …

Layout of business letters and e-mails

A | Introduction

Written communication plays an essential role in business especially in cases where it is important to have a written record of transactions or some form of documentation in writing. In recent years the traditional letter has increasingly been replaced by new, quicker and frequently less formal media. However, in some areas letters are used regularly, for example in legal contexts, in formal contracts and, for example, in the case of serious complaints and reminders. Here the sender may send an email or sometimes a fax in order to speed up matters and then send the same communication by post for the record. It is thus important to be familiar with the standard layout of letters. Although emails are often used because the writer can do without a degree of formality and send them off quickly, in business emails where the partners do not know each other personally the layout and style are more like the body of a letter. Here it is better to be too formal than too informal. When in doubt the many abbreviations used in text messages – also a very useful form of informal written communication – should be avoided in business emails.

B | Model letters and e-mails

1 Model letter (structure)

Here is a letter of a company introducing its services to a customer:

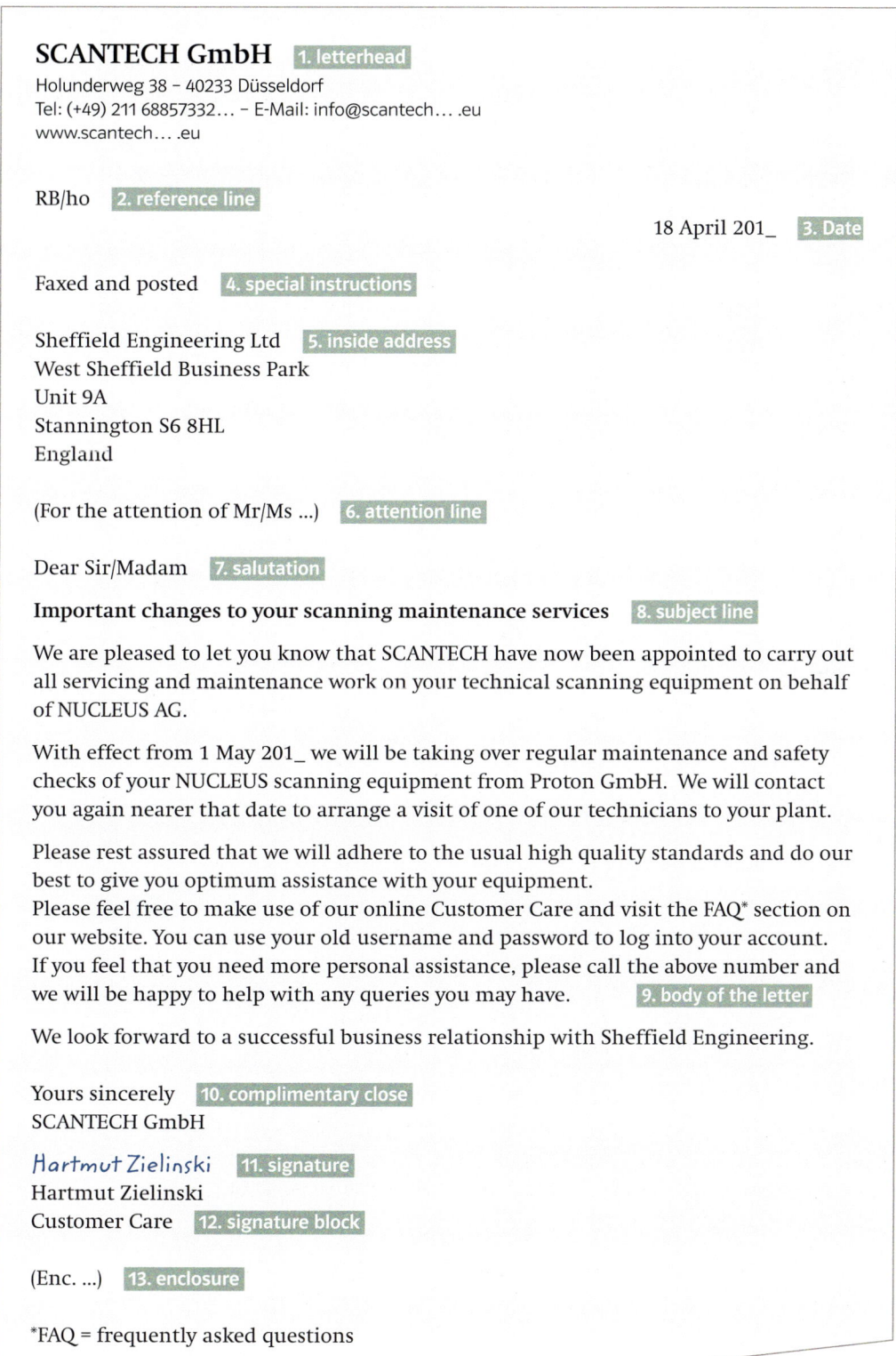

SCANTECH GmbH   1. letterhead
Holunderweg 38 – 40233 Düsseldorf
Tel: (+49) 211 68857332… – E-Mail: info@scantech….eu
www.scantech….eu

RB/ho   2. reference line

18 April 201_   3. Date

Faxed and posted   4. special instructions

Sheffield Engineering Ltd   5. inside address
West Sheffield Business Park
Unit 9A
Stannington S6 8HL
England

(For the attention of Mr/Ms …)   6. attention line

Dear Sir/Madam   7. salutation

Important changes to your scanning maintenance services   8. subject line

We are pleased to let you know that SCANTECH have now been appointed to carry out all servicing and maintenance work on your technical scanning equipment on behalf of NUCLEUS AG.

With effect from 1 May 201_ we will be taking over regular maintenance and safety checks of your NUCLEUS scanning equipment from Proton GmbH. We will contact you again nearer that date to arrange a visit of one of our technicians to your plant.

Please rest assured that we will adhere to the usual high quality standards and do our best to give you optimum assistance with your equipment.
Please feel free to make use of our online Customer Care and visit the FAQ* section on our website. You can use your old username and password to log into your account.
If you feel that you need more personal assistance, please call the above number and we will be happy to help with any queries you may have.   9. body of the letter

We look forward to a successful business relationship with Sheffield Engineering.

Yours sincerely   10. complimentary close
SCANTECH GmbH

Hartmut Zielinski   11. signature
Hartmut Zielinski
Customer Care   12. signature block

(Enc. …)   13. enclosure

*FAQ = frequently asked questions

2 Model e-mail (structure)

From: ruth.bennet@europeansales/the bike factory... .de
To: andrew_simpson@quickmail... .co.uk
Date:
Subject: Start of sales of the Solar Racer e-bike in England
Cc: sales@kent.bicycles... .co.uk
Attachment: Invitation

Dear Mr Simpson   `salutation`

Our new e-bike Solar Racer will be available in England from 1 April 201_
on. We would like to invite you to the official presentation of the Solar
Racer at the Kent Bicycle Shop in Maidstone on 25 March 201_.
Please refer to the attachment.   `body of e-mail`

Kind regards   `complimentary close`

Ruth Bennet   `signature block`
European Sales Manager

The Bike Factory Europe GmbH   `signature footer`
Zwickauer Str. 14 –18
04129 Leipzig
Germany
Tel.: 0049 (0)341 343536-22...
Mobile: 0049 181 75777566...
Fax +49 821 720659...

C | Tool kit

1 Elements of business letters

The **letterhead** shows a company's logo, name, address, telephone and fax
numbers, e-mail and Internet addresses.   `letterhead`

The **reference** may include the initials of the signatory and of the secretary
(e.g. JW/el) or references to files or departments (e.g. Our Ref. D15/a4). Note that
the reference is sometimes preceded by "Ref.", whereas the subject line may be
preceded by "Re:".   `reference`

The date can be written in various different ways: `date`

3 August 201_
3 Aug 201_
3rd August 201_
August 3, 201_
3/8/201_ (BrE) (day/month/year)
8/3/201_ (AmE) (month/day/year)

Obviously, this can easily cause confusion so it is often advisable to write out
the month in full. You should also write out the year in full (i.e. 2015. An
internationally accepted way of writing the date is 2015-08-03 (year-month-day).

The date may be written on the left hand side above the address of the recipient, or on the right in the traditional way.

Special instructions like *Faxed and posted*, *Private and confidential*, or *Urgent*, precede the inside address or the subject line.

special instructions

The **inside address** gives the recipient's full postal address including the country if the letter is going abroad. Note that Messrs, Mrs, Ms, Miss or Mr are written in the same line as the name, not above the name as in Germany. In the USA they are often omitted altogether. The order of the various parts of an address in Britain and the USA is different from that in Germany. Study the following examples:

inside address

Mr Richard Blake AB Filter Technology Ltd 121 Alton Road Guildford GU34 9LZ UK	Elizabeth Elliot Kellynch Components Inc. 1220 Lincoln Avenue Western Springs, IL 60558 USA

Note that Messrs is only used for smaller firms, such as partnerships whose names show that they are not incorporated. Examples:

Messrs J. Vernon & Co.
Messrs Peter Price & Partners
Messrs Jennings & Sons

Messrs is, however, never used for companies that are legal entities in their own right, as shown by the abbreviations "Limited", "Ltd", "Plc" or "plc" after the names of British companies and "Inc." or "Corp." with American companies. Examples:

J. Thorpe Ltd.
J. W. Philips Plc
Robert Osborne Inc.
The Mattress Company

Note that in the UK the post code is written below the place name and in the USA it is written on the same line after the place name, separated by a comma.

"Ms" should be used whenever the marital status of the female addressee is not known. Contrary to German usage, do not address someone as "Mrs" unless you know for certain that she is married.

There is a choice of punctuation in some parts of a letter. The punctuation is either

standard:	open:	US:
David Barratt Ltd. 14, Montpelier Rd., Brighton BN1 2LQ UK	David Barratt Ltd 14 Montpelier Rd Brighton BN1 2LQ UK	Steve Hamilton Capital Supply 3457 Lincoln Av. Des Moines, Iowa 54687 USA
Dear Mr. Barratt,	Dear Mr Barratt	Dear Mr. Hamilton:
Yours sincerely,	Yours sincerely	Sincerely,

Note that in all these cases normal punctuation rules apply to the body of the letter.

An **attention line** ensures that the letter is dealt with by a specific person or – in his or her absence – by a deputy or colleague in charge. You may write "For the attention of Mr John Bull" or "Attention: Miss Jane Doe" or just "Attn. Jane Doe". Alternatively, the name may be included in the inside address.

Traditionally, the **salutation and complimentary close** in business communication must be in line with each other.

`salutation and complimentary close`

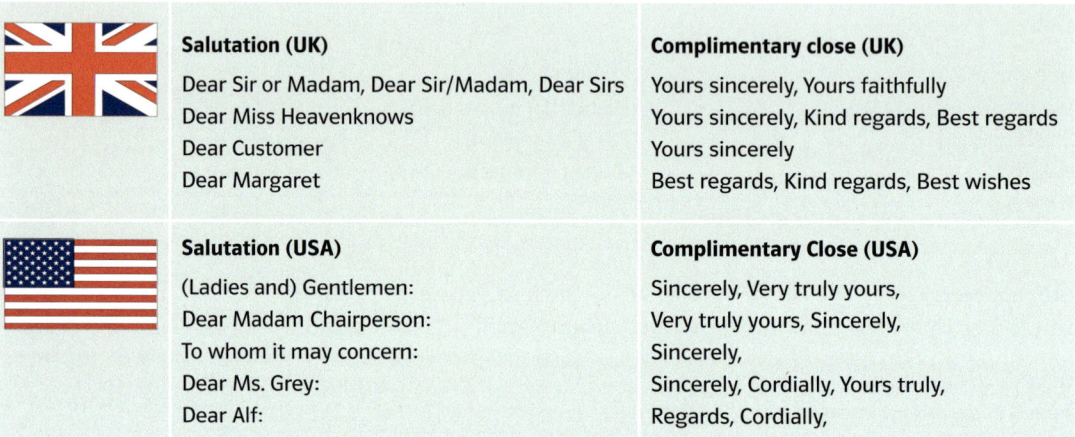

	Salutation (UK)	Complimentary close (UK)
🇬🇧	Dear Sir or Madam, Dear Sir/Madam, Dear Sirs	Yours sincerely, Yours faithfully
	Dear Miss Heavenknows	Yours sincerely, Kind regards, Best regards
	Dear Customer	Yours sincerely
	Dear Margaret	Best regards, Kind regards, Best wishes
	Salutation (USA)	**Complimentary Close (USA)**
🇺🇸	(Ladies and) Gentlemen:	Sincerely, Very truly yours,
	Dear Madam Chairperson:	Very truly yours, Sincerely,
	To whom it may concern:	Sincerely,
	Dear Ms. Grey:	Sincerely, Cordially, Yours truly,
	Dear Alf:	Regards, Cordially,

Nowadays "Yours faithfully" is almost always felt to be too formal and "Yours sincerely" may be used instead. Especially in e-mails and faxes informal endings such as "Best regards" are used.

If at all possible you should address the person you are writing to by name (Dear Mrs McCaghy). "Dear Sir or Madam", "Dear Sir(s)" or "Gentlemen:" is used for initial contact only when you do not have a name to write to.

The **subject line** briefly tells the recipient what the letter, e-mail, fax or memo is about. As it makes things easier for the reader it is also a means of creating goodwill for the sender's firm. This is why most business letters should have a subject line, which may be underlined, or typed in capital letters or bold type. In some firms it is customary to precede the subject line by "Subject:" or "Re:" The subject line should be as specific as possible. Do not just write "Your offer" but "Your offer for mouse pads of 23 March".

`subject line`

In the UK, subject lines are normally, but not always, written below the salutation, in the USA above the salutation.

UK	USA
Dear Ms Shallis	**Your order no. AB/123 for swimwear**
Your Advertisement in The Economist of 2 May 2013	Dear Mr. Leigh:
We are pleased to inform you …	We are sorry to tell you …

Note that in English the first word of the body of the letter has a capital letter.

The **signature block** often begins with the company's name directly below the complimentary close, followed by several blank lines for the signature.

`signature block`

The signatory's name is typed below the signature, and below that his or her position or department are given as well. Women often indicate in brackets behind their name how they wish to be addressed, e.g. Jane Taylor (Mrs).

If somebody signs the letter on behalf of another person, for instance a personal assistant for their boss, their name is typed below the signature, preceded by the word "for" or by the abbreviation "pp.", meaning "on behalf of".

`pp.`

Jane Rushworth
pp. Mary Crawford
Sales Manager

Whenever **enclosures** are sent with a letter, a reference to the enclosure is required at the bottom of the letter. This can take any of the following forms:

`enclosures`

Enc.	Enclosure(s)	Enc.: Invoice No. CB/34	Encs.: 5 Leaflets

Even though actual **carbon copies** are no longer used, the abbreviation cc below the signature is still used to indicate that somebody else is to receive a copy of the letter.

`carbon copies`

cc: William Norris, Chief Financial Officer

2 Elements of e-mails

From:	Your e-mail address will appear automatically.
To:	Be careful not to make the slightest mistake when entering the recipient's address, or else the e-mail will be returned.
Cc:	The abbreviation stands for "carbon copy". With old-style typewriters copies used to be made by inserting carbon paper between the blank sheets of paper.
	This is where you enter the addresses of the persons to whom you wish the message to be forwarded. Bcc (blind copy) is the box where you enter a recipient's name which the other recipients do not see.
Sent:	Instead of "Sent" you may find the word "Date". The correct date and time will be entered automatically.
Attachments:	Any kind of file, such as Word documents (.doc), Excel sheets (.xls), pictures (e. g. .jpg), etc. can be attached to an e-mail.
Subject:	You should always mention the precise subject matter of your correspondence. Firstly it will help your business partner to deal with your mail and secondly it will prevent him/her from deleting it for fear of viruses.
Salutation:	Very formal salutations like "Dear Sir or Madam", "Dear Sirs" or "Gentlemen:" are not used in e-mails. Use "Dear …" instead. In the English-speaking world correspondence is personalised whenever possible: Dear Fiona Dear Ms Starr or even – to avoid "Dear Sirs" or "Dear Sir or Madam" – Dear Sunshine Flights
Complimentary close:	There is a range of expressions to choose from, like With best/kind regards Kind/Best regards/Regards Best wishes or – very formal in e-mails – Yours sincerely

Signature block:	Write your title or department below your name. In Britain women often add (Miss) or (Mrs) in brackets after their name, e. g. Janine Smith (Miss), if they wish to be addressed in this way.
Signature footer:	Add your company's full name, address and telephone number to all e-mails you send to persons or companies who may not know you or your firm.

Do not use special characters like *ß, ä, ö* or *ü*. They may come out very strangely at the other end! Use *ss, ae, oe* and *ue* instead.

Emoticons like :-) for "happy" or ;-) for "only joking" should be reserved for communication with business partners with whom you are on a familiar footing.

⚠ INFO: Netiquette (= (Inter)net etiquette)

– Keep messages short and to the point.
– Focus on one subject per message and include a relevant subject title for the message.
– Include your signature footer when communicating with persons who may not know you personally.
– Capitalise words only to highlight an important point. Capitalising is generally felt to be like SHOUTING!
– Be sparing in your use of exclamation marks.
– Never send chain letters through the Internet.
– Be professional and be careful what you say. E-mails are easily forwarded.
– Be careful when using sarcasm and humour.
– Never assume that your e-mails will be read only by you and the recipient.

---

3 Useful tips: Old-fashioned and modern

Replace old-fashioned expressions by modern equivalents.
This will help to convey the impression of a modern, forward-looking company.

Old-fashioned	Modern
Please be informed that …	We are pleased to inform you …
Please find enclosed …	We are pleased to enclose …/We are enclosing …
As per your request …	As requested …
We are in receipt of …	We have received …
Thanking you in advance we remain …	Thank you for your assistance.

Avoid popular (but wrong) expressions such as "We kindly ask you to …" which must be replaced by "We would like to ask you to …" or by "Please be so kind as to …". The phrase "We like to ask you to …" is also definitely wrong; it should be "We would like to ask you to …".

Telephoning

A | Introduction

Telephoning customers or receiving incoming calls is an important part of business life. Generally it is necessary to use both landlines (fixed lines) and mobile phones. Mobile phones have revolutionised telephone communication, greatly facilitated the ease and speed of business contact and expedited the transaction of business. Many small businesses – sometimes one man or one woman organisations – which cannot afford an expensive office or secretarial back-up rely almost entirely on their mobile or cell phone. They can take calls wherever they happen to be.

However, this technology has not diminished in any way the importance of "telephone manner", i.e. a friendly, helpful and businesslike response with clear enunciation.

When taking messages it is important to make sure that you note down all the relevant details. You should first make sure that you take down the name of the caller. It is usually necessary to ask him/her to spell names and addresses. Be sure to get the postcode.

It is essential to note down telephone numbers accurately. Failure to do so will lead to a lot of problems. Read back telephone numbers to check that you have got them right. Telephone numbers are often read differently in different countries. In Britain numbers are simply given in the order they occur, e.g.: 0044 20 363 2991 = oh oh four four – two oh – three six three – two nine nine (or: double nine) one.

Instead of "oh" Americans usually say "zero". People often say: double oh or: two double nine one. If necessary, ask the caller to repeat the number more slowly. Get callers to spell e-mail addresses precisely. Even the slightest mistake results in e-mails being sent back. "@" is pronounced "at", "." is read as "dot", ("dotcoms" = internet companies), "/" is pronounced "slash" and "–" is read as "hyphen" or "dash" or "minus" and "_" as "underscore". Your company may have a special form for recording telephone messages.

Communication across cultures: Telephoning in English-speaking countries

It is important to use suitable, polite phrases when ringing people in English-speaking countries. If you know the person you are ringing it is usual to ask how they are getting on, etc. before you get down to business (e.g.: "How are you doing? I haven't spoken to you for a long time.").

5 If you are about to mention a problem or difficulty, you should begin with: "I'm afraid ...". A request often begins with: "Could you possibly ...?" ("Could you possibly repeat the address?") or "I would be grateful if you would/could ...". When someone does you a service, it is usual to say something like: "Excellent", or "Brilliant!". When someone thanks you for your help you can

10 say: "You're welcome", or "Not at all".
Don't just say "yes" or "no". Say: "Yes, I think so"; "No, I'm afraid not". The problem for German speakers is that short answers (like "ja" and "nein"), which are NOT impolite in German, come across in English as unfriendly or impolite.

B | Model dialogue

AB = Annegret Berghoff
HL = Heather Lucas
CB = Cyril Brown
NN = unknown person

NN: Hello?
AB: Oh, hello, this is Annegret Berghoff from Schneider GmbH in Braunschweig. Could I speak to Cyril Brown please?
NN: Sorry, you must have dialled the wrong number. This is the Oakleigh nursing home. There's no Cyril here, I'm afraid.
AB: Oh, I'm terribly sorry.
NN: That's alright, dear. (hangs up)
AB: (dials new number)
HL: Good morning, Alba Crystalware, Heather Lucas speaking. How can I help?
AB: Good morning, my name's Annegret Berghoff from Schneider GmbH in Braunschweig. Is Cyril Brown in?
HL: He should be in. Bear with me and I'll try and get hold of him. Just a moment please.
AB: Okay.

HL: He's speaking on the other line. Do you want me to get him to ring you back or would you rather wait?

AB: Erm ... I think I'll wait ... I ...

HL: Oh, hang on. I see he's just finished his call. I'll put you through now.

AB: Thank you.

CB: Good morning Annegret. How are things at your end?

AB: Hello Cyril, fine, thanks. Yourself?

CB: Not too bad. What can I do for you today, Annegret?

AB: Well, the reason I'm calling is your consignment of whisky tumblers, sherry glasses and decanters ...

CB: Which ones? The ones with the Scottish thistle cut?

AB: Yes, those.

CB: Don't tell me they got damaged during transport.

AB: No, no, nothing like that. But we've sold them already and one of our customers needs a set of 50 tumblers, 50 sherry glasses and 10 decanters very urgently. It's to do with a major social event. A golden wedding.

CB: Oh, I see.

AB: How quickly do you think you could supply them?

CB: More or less straight away. They're in stock.

AB: Oh, thank goodness. The event is in two weeks' time, on the 19th. Do you think you'll be able to send the consignment to us before that date?

CB: Oh, certainly. Don't worry. I'll make sure that they get packed and shipped first thing tomorrow morning.

AB: Fantastic, Cyril. There's one more thing. Our customer saw this beautiful crystal bowl from the same Scottish thistle range and asks if it would be possible to have it engraved for that occasion.

CB: Well, if it isn't something terribly difficult ...

AB: He would like to have it engraved with "zur Goldenen Hochzeit für Maria und Wilhelm". The letters should be roughly one centimetre high and in a nice script. Something in the line of Monotype Corsiva.

CB: Yes, I see what you mean. Well, I don't see why that should be a problem. Give us one additional day for that and we'll sort it out.

AB: Brilliant. Shall I spell the text for you?

CB: Yes, please do.

AB: Okay. The first word is small z-u-r. The next word is capital G-o-l-d-e-n-e-n. Then capital H-o-c-h-z-e-i-t.

CB: d for Delta?

AB: No, t for Tango. Then below that small f for Foxtrott, u Umlaut ...

CB: Sorry?

AB: a u with two little dots.

CB: Ah, okay.

AB: r for Romeo. New word. Capital M for Mike, a-r-i-a. New word. Small u-n-d. New word. Capital W-i-l-h-e-l-m.

CB: Okay. I've got that. I'll tell you what Annegret. Before we start engraving the text I'll choose a nice, elegant script and send you an e-mail with the text just to make sure there are no spelling mistakes.

AB: That's an excellent idea, Cyril.

CB: I'll send you the e-mail later today and then you just get back to me and either give your okay or suggest any changes.

AB: Perfect. Thank you so much for your help, Cyril. Talk to you later then. Have a good day.

CB: And you, Annegret. Bye for now.

C | Tool kit

1 Telephone alphabet

When ringing people in other countries it is often necessary to spell unfamiliar words, names and addresses, e-mail addresses, etc. and give punctuation. It is possible to use the international alphabet given below. There are, however, other popular alphabets in use and people often make up their own as they go along.

International telephone alphabet

There is an International Telephone Alphabet which is used to avoid misunderstandings:

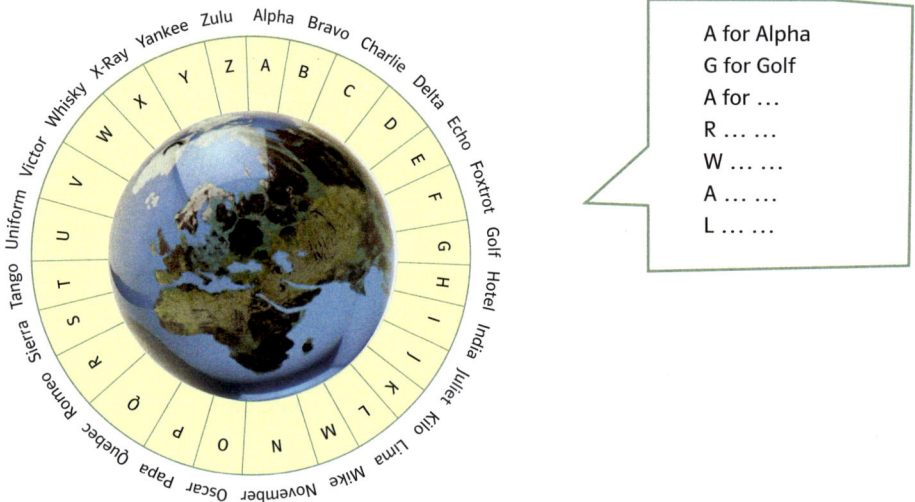

A for Alpha
G for Golf
A for …
R … …
W … …
A … …
L … …

Informal telephone alphabet

People in Britain often either make it up or use the following alphabet:

Andrew	George	Lucy	Queenie	Victor
Benjamin	Harry	Mary	Robert	William
Charlie	Isaac	Nelly	Sugar	Xmas
David	Jack	Oliver	Tom	Yellow
Edward	King	Peter	Uncle	Zebra
Frederick				

The main thing is that you should have English words or names at your fingertips in case you are asked to spell something over the phone.

2 Punctuation

Remember the most important punctuation marks:

.	full stop	Punkt
.	dot	Punkt in E-Mail-Adressen
,	comma	Komma
;	semi-colon	Strichpunkt

:	colon	Doppelpunkt
?	question mark	Fragezeichen
'	apostrophe	Apostroph
!	exclamation mark	Ausrufezeichen
@	at	(in E-Mail-Adressen)
/	slash	Schrägstrich
\	backslash	Backslash
-	hyphen	Bindestrich
-	hyphen/dash/minus	Bindestrich in E-Mail-Adressen
—	dash	Gedankenstrich
1_a	underscore/understroke	Unterstreichungszeichen (tiefer Bindestrich in E-Mail-Adressen)
(…)	in brackets	in Klammern
[ ]	square brackets	eckige Klammern
(	open bracket	Klammer auf
)	close bracket	Klammer zu
"…"	quotation marks/inverted commas	Anführungszeichen
"…	quote	Anführungszeichen vorne
…"	unquote	Anführungszeichen hinten
#	hash	Raute

Note also when spelling:

– Großbuchstaben/Kleinbuchstaben = **capitals/small letters** or **upper case/lower case letters**
– ö, ä, ü = **o, a, u-Umlaut** or **o, a, u with two dots**

3 Dictation

When someone dictates a text they have to provide additional information so that it can be typed correctly. Here are the most important words and phrases for dictating.

Phrases/Advice	**Comments**
Please take a dictation. Address it to … Put today's date and our reference …	Spell the name and the address of the recipient if you are not sure that the secretary can type it correctly.
Dear M … – comma, new paragraph. Thank you for your enquiry of 3 October – full stop, new paragraph.	In the dictation tell the secretary where to put the punctuation marks and where to begin a new paragraph.
Europe – capital E POWERCOMP – in capital letters	Also indicate a word that begins with a capital letter or is entirely in CAPITAL LETTERS.
Yours sincerely – comma, new paragraph – my name and job title.	Before you finish, give instructions as to signature, name and job title and other relevant items.
We are enclosing our latest price list.	Mention the enclosure(s).

4 Useful telephone phrases

To make friendly remarks at the beginning of a telephone conversation	Reactions
Oh, hello Sarah. Nice to hear from you. How are things over there?	Just fine, thank you.
Good morning Mrs Weston. I hope you enjoyed your holiday.	Thank you, it was very relaxing.
Good afternoon Mr Fraser. How is the weather in Scotland?	We've had a lot of snow recently.

To ask for somebody	To say that somebody isn't available
Could I speak to Mrs Foster?	I'm afraid Mrs Foster isn't in.
Could you put me through to Ms King?	
I'd like to speak to someone from the sales department.	… is in a meeting.
	… has a visitor.
	… is in the USA on a business trip.
	… is out at lunch.
	… is no longer with our company.

To offer to ring back or take a message	Reactions
I'm afraid Mrs Foster is speaking on the other line.	Thank you, I'll ring back later.
Would you prefer to wait or shall I ask her to ring you back?	I'm afraid I won't be in this afternoon. Tomorrow morning would be better.
Can she call you back this afternoon?	Yes, that would be best. Could you tell her that …?
Can I give her a message?	Yes, please. Could you take the following message: …
Would you like to leave a message?	

To refer somebody to someone else		Reactions
I'm afraid I'm not	familiar with that order.	Thank you.
	in charge of this transaction. I'll put you through to Mr Croft.	
Shall I put you through to Mrs Lucas? Perhaps she can help you.		No, thanks. I really need to speak to the export manager.
Would you like to speak to somebody from the accounts department?		

To ask for something	Reactions
Would you please let me know if …?	Yes, of course.
I'd like to ask you whether it would be possible to …	We'll do our best, but …
You'd be doing us a great favour if you could …	You may depend on it.
Please make sure that …	Certainly.
We must ask you to remit the invoice amount by Friday at the latest.	

To refuse something

- I'm afraid I cannot agree to that proposal.
- I'm afraid that sounds quite/totally unacceptable to us.
- Much as I regret it, I have to say no.
- I'm terribly sorry, but I simply can't see any way of making this concession.
- Unfortunately, this is not what we had in mind.

Reactions

- That's too bad.
- I'm sorry to hear that.
- Well, I'm afraid there's nothing to be done.
- Is there nothing you can do?

To apologise

- I'm terribly sorry but …
- I'd like to apologise for the trouble you've been having.
- Please accept our apologies.
- I can only repeat that I am extremely sorry for what has happened.

Reactions

- It's alright, don't mention it.
- Well, please try to avoid this happening in future. It has caused us a lot of problems.

To play for time

| Can I ring you back? | I need to study our files first. |
| | I must discuss the matter with the head of department. |

- I'm afraid I can't access the file on my monitor right now. I'll call you back in half an hour.
- I'd rather not rush things. I'll get back to you after 5 pm if that's alright. I'll have more time then to discuss the matter.
- Let's deal with one point at a time.
- I suggest we think the problem over for a few more days.

Reactions

- I'm afraid I am not prepared to be put off again.
- I insist on speaking to the person responsible.
- That's a good idea.
- I totally agree with you.

To make an appointment

- Would it be possible for you to meet me at the Boat Fair?
- Would Tuesday suit you?
- I'm free on 22 May all afternoon.
- Couldn't we switch the appointment to the next morning, say at 10:30?
- What about postponing the meeting to the last week in May?

Reactions

- Certainly. I'll be there on Wednesday.
- I'm afraid Tuesday is full.
- I'm afraid I've got an appointment at that time.
- That would be alright with me.
- Yes, Wednesday would be fine.
- On 22 May at 3 pm then.

To request that something is done by a certain date

- We need the goods by Wednesday at the very latest.
- I repeat, we require the documents by 3 May.

- Please make sure that it arrives no later than the end of April.
- Monday, 31 July is the final deadline.

To promise something

- We promise you that …
- You have my word, the documents will reach you on Monday.
- We will certainly see to it that …

- You may rely on it, the goods will be dispatched tomorrow.

To end the telephone conversation	Reactions
Goodbye Mrs Benwick. Thanks for calling.	You're very welcome. Goodbye.
Goodbye Mr Hayter. Have a nice weekend.	You too, Mrs Dalrymple.

5 Typical phrases (German/English): Telephoning

1. Wie schön, dass ich Sie erreicht habe. Wie geht's Ihnen?	Nice to hear from you. How are things over there?
2. Wie ist denn das Wetter bei Ihnen? Hier regnet es seit Wochen.	How's the weather over there? Over here it's been raining for weeks.
3. Könnten Sie mich mit Mrs. Bennet aus der Export-abteilung verbinden?	Could you put me through to Mrs Bennet from the export department?
4. Soll ich ihm etwas ausrichten oder soll er Sie zurückrufen?	Can I give him a message or shall I ask him to ring you back?
5. Ich bin da nicht zuständig. Soll ich Sie zu Frau Neff durchstellen?	I'm afraid I'm not in charge of this transaction. Shall I put you through to Mrs Neff?
6. Würden Sie mich bitte benachrichtigen, wenn …	Would you please let me know if …
7. Bitte kümmern Sie sich darum, dass …	Please make sure that …
8. Damit können wir uns leider nicht einverstanden erklären.	I'm afraid we cannot agree to that.
9. So hatten wir uns das nicht gedacht.	Unfortunately, this is not what we had in mind.
10. Bitte entschuldigen Sie die Verzögerung.	Please accept our apologies for the delay.
11. Es tut mir schrecklich leid, aber …	I'm terribly sorry but …
12. Kann ich Sie zurückrufen, ich muss erst in den Unterlagen nachsehen?	Can I ring you back? I need to study the files first.
13. Wir wollen doch nichts überstürzen.	We had better not rush things.
14. Eins nach dem andern.	Let's deal with one point at a time.
15. Das sollten wir erst einmal überschlafen.	I suggest we think the problem over for a day or two.
16. Könnten wir uns nicht auf der Buchmesse treffen?	Would it be possible for you to meet me at the Book Fair?
17. Mir wäre es lieb, wenn wir den Termin um eine Woche verschieben könnten.	Couldn't we postpone the appointment by one week?
18. Der Bericht muss spätestens Donnerstag vorliegen.	We need the report by Thursday at the latest.
19. Vielen Dank für Ihren Anruf.	Thanks for calling.
20. Auf Wiederhören	Goodbye.

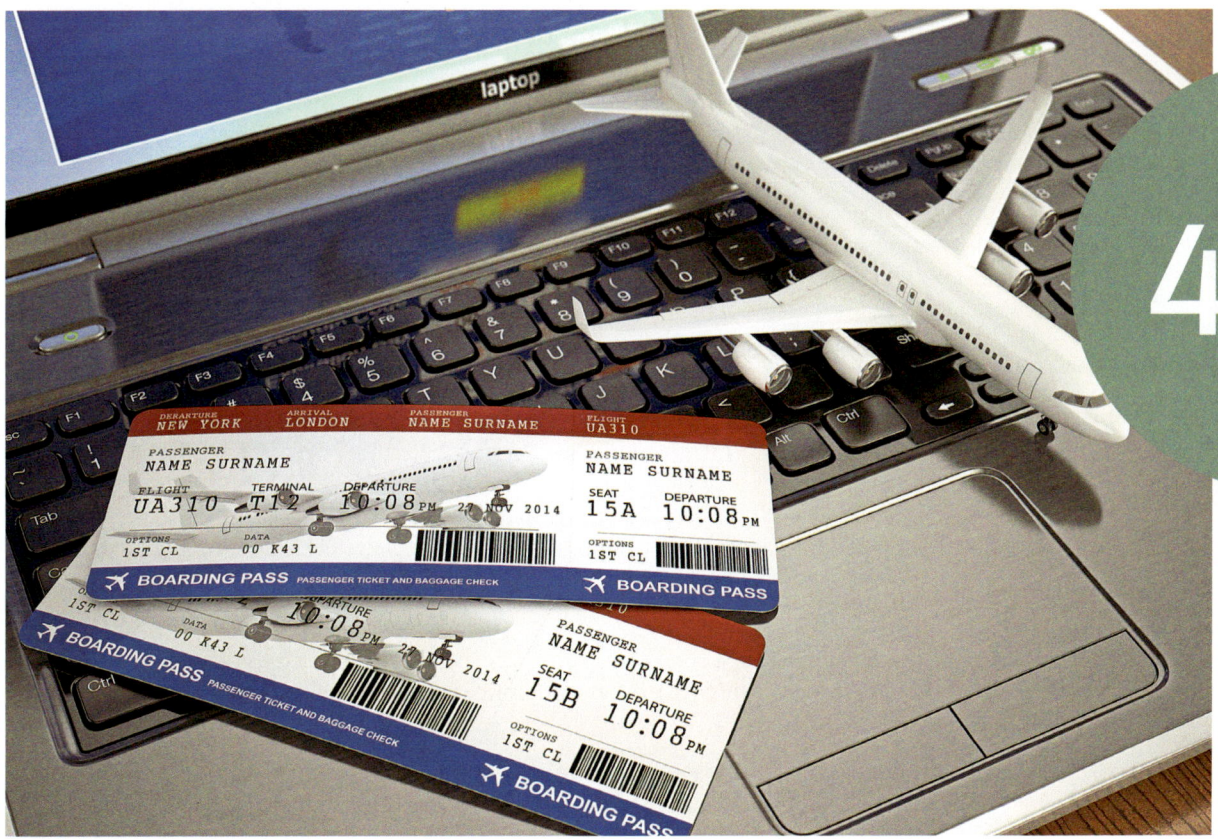

Making arrangements

A | Introduction

An important part of the job of PAs, (personal assistants), secretaries and clerical staff is to make arrangements on behalf of management. This will include booking flights, making hotel reservations, hiring cars, reserving exhibition space, etc. They may also be required to organise meetings and conferences and to take part in order to keep the minutes and generally facilitate proceedings.

One of the duties of a PA or secretary is to welcome visitors and make them feel at home. It may be necessary to entertain them until the person they have arranged to see arrives. The language in which you and they can communicate will often be English, even when the visitors do not come from an English-speaking country. Today, almost everywhere in the world English is used as the lingua franca of business.

B | Model e-mails and model telephone dialogue

1 Invitations

1.1 Writing an invitation:

Cambridge Association of Information Technology
33 Newmarket Rd, Cambridge CB5 8LI
www.cait.org....uk

13 May 201_

Webmaster GmbH
Glashüttenweg 78
07741 Jena
Germany

INVITATION – CONFERENCE ON NEW DEVELOPMENTS IN E-COMMERCE

Dear Sir/Madam,

As a major German supplier of e-commerce solutions you will be pleased to know that the CAIT is organising its annual conference in Cambridge on new developments in e-commerce.

The topics discussed will include new software developments, important changes in EU legislation and the adaptation of marketing strategies to an increasingly heterogeneous business environment.

This conference will provide valuable information and a discussion forum for businesses involved in e-commerce and give you the opportunity to meet new customers and exchange views with business partners and IT specialists in this field

The event will take place on Saturday, 10 July 201_, from 9am to 5pm at our convention centre in Newmarket Road, Cambridge.

We can organise accommodation for you at the William & Mary Hotel which is adjacent to our centre. As we expect a large number of participants we would ask you to let us know asap if you are interested in attending the conference and whether you want us to book a room/rooms for you at the hotel. Please send us an e-mail to bookings@cait.org.uk giving your details (dates of arrival and departure, number of persons, special requirements).

We look forward to welcoming you to our conference in July.

Yours sincerely,

Anna Zilbermann
Anna Zilberman
PR-Manager

Encs: hotel brochure and price list
       location map
       conference programme

1.2 Accepting an invitation:

From: j.bucholtz@webmaster... .eu
To: bookings@cait.org... .uk
Sent: 16 May 201_
Subject: Your invitation of 13 May

Dear Ms Zilberman,

Thank you very much for your invitation to take part in this year's conference on new developments in e-commerce.

I am pleased to let you know that I would like to attend the conference and would ask you to book a double room at the William & Mary Hotel for me and my wife. We would need accommodation incl. breakfast for 3 nights. We would arrive in Cambridge on Friday, 9 July, and depart on the following Monday.

Please send me an e-mail confirming my reservation for the conference and your hotel booking.

I look forward to seeing you in July.

Kind regards,
Joachim Bucholtz
Sales and Marketing
Webmaster GmbH

1.3 Declining an invitation:

From: k.kleinen@cybersolutions... .de
To: bookings@cait.org... .uk
Sent: 16 May 201_
Subject: Your invitation of 13 May

Dear Ms Zilberman,

Thank you very much for your invitation to take part in this year's CAIT conference in Cambridge.

Much as I would have liked to come to Cambridge on 10 July, I will unfortunately not be able to attend the conference this year as I will be in Portugal that weekend advising a customer on some of our latest products.

I would, however, appreciate it very much if you could keep me up to date re any upcoming CAIT events as I find them an invaluable source of information and an excellent platform to establish new contacts.

I wish you much success with your conference and hope to hear from you again soon.

Best regards,
Klemens Kleinen
Sales and Marketing
Cyber Solutions KG

2 Bookings

2.1 Booking an exhibition stand

KS = Katrin Stauder
IC = Indira Chaudhary
R = Reception

KS: Good morning. I'm ringing from Leipzig in Germany. I want to check our reservation. Could you put me through to the person or department in charge of stand reservations, please?

R: Certainly madam. Could you give me the name of your company?

KS: The company is Universal Box plc.

R: Excellent. I'm putting you through to the stand reservations department.

IC: Good morning, Indira Chaudhary speaking. How can I help you?

KS: Hello. My name is Katrin Stauder from Universal Box plc, Leipzig subsidiary. I booked a stand three months ago but have not yet received confirmation.

IC: Oh yes, it rings a bell. Just a moment, please. Yes, I can see on my monitor that the stand – corner stand 25 m^2 with kitchenette and partitioned conference area has been reserved.

KS: Brilliant. Could you possibly send me an email confirming this?

IC: Certainly, madam. Could you give me your email address, please?

KS: It is ks.universalboxplc@t-online.de – ks-dot-universalboxplc as one word @ t-online.de

AP: Good, I'll send that off immediately.

2.2 Enquiring about a booking on the phone

Joachim Bucholtz of Webmaster GmbH in Jena booked a stand at the International Electronics Fair in Tel Aviv. He has received confirmation of the booking, but is still waiting for some important information from the fair organisers. He decides to ring them up to discuss the issue.

JB = Joachim Bucholtz
EB = Esther Siskind

EB: Good morning, Tel Aviv Convention Centre, Esther Siskind speaking. How can I help?

JB: Good morning. My name is Joachim Bucholtz from Webmaster in Jena, Germany. I'm calling about the International Electronics Fair in October.

EB: Yes, what can I help you with, Mr Bucholtz?

JB: Well, we booked a stand a couple of weeks ago. I've received confirmation of the booking, but I'm still waiting for details from the stand constructors.

EB: Do you have your booking number handy, Mr Bucholtz?

JB: I do. It's 67/HT/8091.

EB: Just a second, Mr Bucholtz. I'll just check if there is any information coming up on our system. Oh, yes, here we are. Webmaster GmbH. You reserved floor space for a stand of 8 times 10 metres in the main exhibition hall, is that correct?

JB: Yes, that's correct.

EB: I see that you sent us your specifications for the stand and we contacted our contractors who are in charge of stand construction. It seems everything has gone through. Haven't they been in touch with you?

JB: No, that's why I'm a bit worried. After all, the fair is in 6 weeks' time.

EB: You're quite right. I'll tell you what I'll do. I'll put you through to our contractor in Haifa. The person in charge is Leigh Parris. I'm sure he'll be able to help you. Hold the line, while I connect you.

JB: Thank you very much for your help, Ms Siskind.

EB: You're very welcome, Mr Bucholtz. Have a good day.

JB: And you. Good-bye.

2.3 Confirming a booking:

From: bookings@cait.org... .uk
To: j.bucholtz@webmaster... .eu
Sent: 17 May 201_
Re: Confirmation of hotel booking and participation at conference
Attachment: Booking confirmation

Dear Mr Bucholtz,

I am delighted that you will be able to attend our conference this summer and very much look forward to welcoming you and your wife to Cambridge.

As instructed, I have booked a double room for 3 nights incl. breakfast at the William & Mary Hotel for the duration of your stay. Please find attached the booking confirmation of the hotel.

Please do not hesitate to contact me if you have any queries or anything else I can help you with to make your stay as enjoyable as possible.

Best wishes,
Anna Zilberman
PR-Manager

C | Tool kit

1 Useful phrases for welcoming a visitor

Good morning. Can I help you?

I'm afraid Frau Wagner hasn't got here yet. She's probably been held up by the traffic.

I'm expecting her to arrive at any moment.

Herr Kramer is sorry to keep you waiting.

He'll be here in about five minutes.

I've been trying to contact Frau Dr Kaiser on her mobile.

Would you like to take a seat? I'll tell Frau Dr Kaiser you've arrived.

Herr Friedrichs will be down in a moment.

I'm afraid Frau Weinhold is not at her desk. I shall have to ring round to find out where she is. It shouldn't take more than a moment.

Herr Friedrichs is expecting you.

The weather is ghastly, isn't it?

This is the first warm spring day we've had.

Have you got a heat wave like this in England?

What's the weather like in South Africa at this time of the year?

Can I get you anything? Would you like some tea or coffee?

I hope you had a pleasant journey/flight.

Is this your first visit to Berlin?

I hope that your hotel is comfortable.

It is very convenient for the city centre.

Perhaps you would prefer to wait in the visitors' lounge until Frau Dr Kaiser gets here. Would you like the Financial Times?

Would you just come this way, please?

I'll let you know the minute Herr von Ranzau gets here.

Is there anything else I could get you?

2 Building blocks: Secretarial communication

To enquire about, reserve, book or cancel hotel and conference rooms

				for non-smokers.
Please reserve for us We require We would like to book	a single room a double room an executive suite a self-catering flat	with	bath shower and WC en suite facilities.	
			on a different floor. facing the sea. and parking facilities for 2 cars.	

for	one of our senior executives Mr Cole, our service engineer, a group of representatives	**for**	three nights **from** 3 **to** 6 March. the duration of the trade fair. a period of at least 6 weeks.	

For …	we need …	equipped with …
our annual general meeting a meeting of our distributors a project conference	an assembly hall of at least 500 square metres a conference room seating about 50 persons a quiet meeting room	flip chart. computer projector. an interactive whiteboard. all the usual facilities. a stage and a big screen.

Coffee, tea and soft drinks will be required at all times during the meeting.

A buffet lunch would be appreciated.

Lunch will have to be served at 12:30.

We regret having to	change cancel	the reservation the booking	**at** such short notice. because Mrs Osborne is unable to get a flight for that date. due to circumstances beyond our control.

To book flights and reserve train tickets

You are booked **on** flight no. LH 348, leaving Heathrow **at** 17:15, arriving (**at** the airport) **in** Cologne **at** 20:10 **on** 23 March.

Please reserve two seats for us	by the window next to the aisle adjacent to each other	in a first class carriage.

To write invitations

The chairman	will be pleased to welcome you **at** invites you to attend	our annual dinner **at** the Park Hotel. a conference **on** the prospects of e-commerce.
	is looking forward to meeting you for an informal discussion **in** the VIP lounge.	

The	meeting reception presentation	will be held will take place	**at** the King George Hotel **at** the Conference Centre **in** our main hall	**on** Wednesday, June 7th. **from** 7 pm **to** 9 pm. **between** 10 am **and** 3 pm.

3 Building blocks: Fairs and exhibitions

To ask the organisers for information

We are interested in	introducing our software solutions displaying our latest innovations exhibiting our products	at	this year's PC Fair the Melbourne Fair the Motor Show in Detroit

and would ask you to send us	your information package with application forms. information on your rates and deadlines. names and addresses of stand-constructors.

To book space or a stand

Our company wishes	to book a stand in the main exhibition hall. to reserve floor space for a stand covering 8 x 15 metres. to rent an outdoor area of about 250 square metres.

To organise the necessary equipment

Our stand must be equipped with	a hot and cold water supply. telephone and ISDN lines. 220 Volt sockets.

Competent interpreters (English/German) First-class catering services 4 small tables and 16 upholstered chairs	will also be required.

To have a stand built and dismantled

Are you in a position to	build a stand for us according to the enclosed specifications?
	design an eye-catching stand for us and erect it before May 15?
	help us remove the heavy exhibits and dismantle the stand?

4 Typical phrases (German/English): Making arrangements

	German	English
1.	Da wir unsere Produkte auch dieses Jahr auf der Industriemesse in Shanghai ausstellen möchten, bitten wir Sie um Zusendung der Anmeldeformulare, Tarife und Bedingungen.	As we would like to exhibit our products at the industrial fair in Shanghai this year, we would ask you to send us application forms and information on tariffs and conditions.
2.	Unser Stand soll sich im Zentrum von Halle 8 befinden und mit Internetanschluss ausgestattet sein.	We would prefer a stand with internet access, located at the centre of hall 8.
3.	Könnten Sie uns zwei kompetente Dolmetscherinnen und ein zuverlässiges Verpflegungsunternehmen empfehlen?	Could you recommend two competent interpreters and a reliable catering service?
4.	Ich benötige ein ruhiges Einzelzimmer mit Bad sowie einen Parkplatz in der Hotelgarage vom 27. bis 31. Juli.	I need a quiet single room with bath as well as parking space in the hotel car park from 27 to 31 July.
5.	Der Konferenzraum muss mit Whiteboard und Beamer ausgestattet sein.	The conference room must be equipped with a computer projector and a DVD player.
6.	Da für den 27. August alle Flüge ausgebucht waren, müssen wir die Reservierung des Einzelzimmers für Frau Stellfeld leider ändern. Sie wird erst am 28. anreisen und, wie vorgesehen, am 30. abreisen.	As there was no flight available on 27 August we regret having to change the booking for Mrs Stellfeld. She will be arriving on 28 August and leaving on 30 August, as planned.
7.	Wir geben uns die Ehre, Sie zu unserem Neujahrsempfang am 9. Januar um 18 Uhr im Hotel Superior einzuladen.	We will be pleased to welcome you at our New Year reception at the Hotel Superior on 9 January at 18:00.
8.	Bitte reservieren Sie für mich einen Platz am Gang in einem Großraumwagen der 1. Klasse.	Please reserve an aisle seat for me in a first class saloon carriage.
9.	Ihr Flug ist BA 1024, Abflug 13:30 Uhr von Köln/Bonn, Ankunft 15:20 Uhr in Oslo.	Your flight is BA 1024, departure time 13:30 from Cologne/Bonn airport, arrival time 15:20 in Oslo.
10.	Ich benötige einen Beamer für die Präsentation.	I will need a computer projector for my presentation.

Enquiries

A | Introduction

Business transactions often start with an enquiry. An enquiry may be
– general, i.e. a request for sales literature, price lists, etc. or
– more specific seeking information about goods or services required or
– requesting a detailed quotation including terms of payment, delivery
  periods and any (introductory) discounts.

There are several ways for potential customers to obtain the information
they require:
1. ring the supplier or send a text message
2. email the company
3. write a letter of enquiry
4. occasionally send a fax

However, the internet and company websites are often the most convenient way
of locating suppliers while trade fairs, exhibitions and advertising campaigns
provide information on new products.

B | Model enquiries by e-mail and on the phone

1 Enquiry by e-mail/letter (structure)

The following is the body of a letter or an e-mail sent to enquire about a company's services. It shows the general structure of an enquiry.

...

Opening event of our new academy   1. subject line

Dear Ms Ohrt,   2. appropriate salutation

My name is Erik Johansson and I'm the Marketing Manager of the Swedish division of LINGOPRO, one of the leading international business colleges with academies throughout Europe.   3. introduction of the firm

I came across "Yay! Event Management" when I visited the "Instructo" education fair in Malmö last April and was very impressed by the range of services you offer.   4. source of address

LINGOPRO will be expanding its Swedish business activities and open a new academy in Lund in September. We therefore require the expertise of a professional event manager to help us make the launch of the new school a great success. We are planning an opening event with presentations, workshops and – of course – a lot of entertainment, food and drinks. Prior to the event we need to make sure that our activities comply with Swedish health and safety regulations.   5. reason for enquiry

If you are interested in organising the event for us, I would be grateful if we could discuss the details via online video chat. I will be available all day (9am to 6pm) Monday to Friday this week. Could you send me a quick reply and let me know what day/time would be most convenient for you?
6. request for quick reply

I look forward to hearing from you.   7. closing phrase

Best regards   8. complimentary close

Erik Johannson
Marketing Manager
LINGOPRO

---

2 Enquiry by telephone

The export manager of a German manufacturer of precision tools is looking for a language school in Britain to improve the English language skills of the people working in his department. He has found the advertisement of a school in Bournemouth in a German newspaper and decides to ring them and enquire about details of language classes.

HS = Hans Schilling
TS = person on telephone switchboard
KL = Karen Longman

TS: Dorset Language School, good afternoon, how can I help?

HS: Good morning, my name is Hans Schilling from Acerofin in Stuttgart, Germany. I'm calling because I saw your advertisement in a German daily newspaper and I am interested in learning a bit more about your language classes.

TS: Certainly, Mr Schilling. I'll put you through to Karen Longman who is in charge of customer care. Just a second please. Hold the line.

HS: Thank you.
(music playing)

KL: Hello, Mr Schilling, sorry for keeping you waiting.

HS: That's alright.

KL: Our receptionist told me that you're interested in our language classes.

HS: Yes, that's right.

KL: Is that for yourself?

HS: No, actually I'm looking for a language class for our staff in the export department. We are a small manufacturer of precision tools located in Stuttgart in southern Germany and we have an increasing number of English-speaking customers. So I thought it might be a good idea to improve the language skills of our personnel.

KL: That's an excellent idea, Mr Schilling. Do the members of your staff have any previous knowledge of English or are they absolute beginners?

HS: Well, they all speak and understand a little English. You, know, school English. But I feel it's not enough to communicate with our customers.

KL: Right. Well, we offer a wide range of classes from beginners and intermediate learners to advanced students. What we usually do before allocating students to specific classes is to assess them.

HS: Do you mean, give them a test?

KL: That's right. One of our teachers will have a short interview with them and then they'll be given a a series of tasks. This enables us to put them into the group that best suits their level.

HS: I see.

KL: How many people will there be in that group? Or were you thinking of individual, one-to-one tuition.

HS: There are five people. If at all possible I would prefer them to be taught in one group.

KL: Certainly. And the group size means we can organise a small, flexible class and make sure that the students get the best out of the lessons. What about the time frame and the number of lessons? What did you have in mind?

HS: Would it be possible to organise a class for 3 weeks from mid-August to early September? I was thinking of 4 or 5 hours Mondays to Fridays. That would give my staff enough time to relax a bit and enjoy the seaside.

KL: Absolutely.

HS: Do you also provide accommodation?

KL: We don't, but we can arrange accommodation at a very nice, quiet hotel near the college.

HS: That sounds perfect. Could you send me your brochure giving all the relevant details, including your price list and a booking form?

KL: I certainly can, Mr Schilling. I'll arrange for everything to be sent out to you first thing tomorrow morning.

HS: Brilliant. Let me give you our address. Our company is called Acerofin. That is spelled A-C-E-R-O-F-I-N.

KL: M for Mike?

HS: No, N for November. The address is Leonberger Allee 129 in 70616 Stuttgart. Shall I spell that for you?

KL: I can spell Stuttgart. A friend of mine actually lives there. But you'll have to help me with the street. So, Leonberger Allee. Is that L-E-O-N-B-E-R-G-E-R?

HS: That's correct. Then new word: A-double L-double E.

KL: Yes, got that. Can you give me your contact telephone number and e-mail address?

HS: Sure. It's 0049 – that's the code for Germany – and then 711 for Stuttgart and 886 736 90. My e-mail address is: Schilling, S-C-H-I-double L-I-N-G, minus H-A-N-S at T minus online dot D-E.

KL: Thank you very much, Mr Schilling. Our information pack should be in your post in a couple of days.

HS: Thanks a lot, Ms Longman. I'll get back to you very shortly.

KL: It was very nice talking to you, Mr Schilling. Have a good day.

HS: And you. Bye for now.

KL: Bye.

C | Tool kit

1 Building blocks for business communications: Enquiries

To mention the source of address

We saw	your advertisement **for**	your office chairs	in your online newsletter.
We refer to	your description **of**		in the May issue of "Furniture World".

We have obtained	your address **from**	the Anglo-German Chamber of Commerce.
		an online business directory.
		the Indian Consulate in Munich.

Your	products have been	recommended **to** us by one of our business partners.
	services have been	
	company has been	

We have visited your website and …

We saw your products at the Machine Tools Exhibition in Leeds.

To introduce your business

We are		company enterprise business	manufacturing specialising **in** distributing offering

Our company is a We are a	major fast-growing successful leading	supplier of … distributor of … wholesaler of … importer of … chain of fashion retailers.

To explain the reason for your enquiry

As there is		on the local market in Germany all over the EU

we are interested **in**	marketing importing distributing selling	the following articles: your products. a selection of … first-class …

To say what you require

Please Would you please	email us let us have send us attach	an offer **for** a quotation **for** a brochure describing a catalogue **of** sales literature **on** the current price list **for** detailed information **on**	your most recent model. the products you import. your Indian spices.
		a cost estimate for	the performance of … the services you offer.

To ask for information

We	require would be grateful for	details **of** information **on**	your the	prices and discounts. terms of payment and delivery. delivery periods. quantities available.

What are your terms of payment?
Do you grant any quantity discounts?
Can you deliver ex stock?

To ask for other services, if applicable

○ A visit **by** your representative	
○ A demonstration **on** our premises	would be appreciated.
○ A presentation of your services	

To close the communication with a standard phrase

If your prices are competitive, we may be able to place substantial orders in the near future.
We hope to **hear** from you shortly.

We	○ are looking forward	**to**	○ hear**ing** from you soon.
	○ look forward		○ an early reply.

2 Typical phrases (German/English): Enquiries

1. Bitte senden Sie uns Prospektmaterial für Ihre neuesten Modelle.	Please send us sales literature on your latest models.
2. Wir sind ein mittelständisches Unternehmen, spezialisiert auf den Vertrieb von hochwertigen Lederwaren.	We are a medium-sized company, specializing in the distribution of upmarket leather goods.
3. Wir sind ein führendes Importunternehmen für exotische Gewürze.	We are a leading importer of exotic spices.
4. Wir haben die ausführliche Beschreibung ihrer Bürostühle in Ihrem Online-Newsletter gelesen.	We have read the detailed description of your swivel chairs in your online newsletter.
5. Wir wären dankbar für die Zusendung von Prospekten und Preislisten.	We would ask you to send us brochures and price lists.
6. Wir haben Ihre Anschrift vom indischen Konsulat in München erhalten.	We obtained your address from the Indian Consulate in Munich.
7. Bitte geben Sie uns Auskunft über Ihre Liefer- und Zahlungsbedingungen.	Please inform us about your terms of delivery and payment.
8. Wir sehen Ihrer baldigen Antwort mit Interesse entgegen.	We are looking forward to your early reply.
9. Ihr Unternehmen wurde uns von Knightley Ltd in Leeds empfohlen.	Your firm has been recommended to us by Knightley Ltd. in Leeds.
10. Könnte uns ihr Vertreter im Lauf der nächsten Woche besuchen?	10. Could your representative visit us in the course of next week?
11. Wir bitten Sie um einen Kostenvoranschlag für die Durchführung der Malerarbeiten.	11. A cost estimate for the paint work would be appreciated.
12. Bitte teilen Sie uns Ihre kürzeste Lieferzeit mit.	12. What is your shortest delivery time?

3 Structural elements of business correspondence

Business communications should have a clear structure consisting of three
essential parts – the beginning, the main part and the end.

The **beginning** is either a single sentence or a brief paragraph. It states the
reason why you are writing.

Example: We wish to inform you that there has been a delay in the shipment
of the MF2GD Spray Dryer.

The **main part** (middle) contains the details. If there are two important points,
there should be two paragraphs.

Example: According to the terms of the contract the spray dryer was to be
delivered no later than 20 Aug 201_. However, there has been no delivery as yet.
If there is a reason for the delay, please let us know. We would also like to know
if there is a revised delivery date.

If we incur damages due to further delay in delivering the spray dryer, we
will advise you of them. We likewise wish to remind you of the penalty clause of
$500.00 per day for failure to deliver on time.

The **end section** sums up what has been said and underlines the expectations
of the writer towards the recipient.

Example: Please let us have your reactions as soon as possible in this matter.

The end section often also contains a sentence intended to create good will.

Example: We look forward to doing business with you and feel sure that you
will be satisfied with our services.

D | Avoiding common mistakes

Wrong	Correct
1. Enquiry ~~for~~	1. Enquiry **about**
2. You have been ~~recommended us~~ by …	2. You have been recommended **to** us by …
3. We are ~~specialised~~ in …	3. We are **specialising in** …/We **specialise in** …
4. A ~~mayor~~ supplier	4. A major supplier
5. We are ~~interesting~~ in …	5. We are **interested in** …
6. An offer ~~about~~ …	6. An offer **for** …
7. Please send us a ~~prospect~~.	7. Please send us a **brochure/catalogue.**
8. We are sending you by ~~seperate~~ mail …	8. We are sending you by **separate** mail …
9. ~~How~~ are your terms of payment?	9. **What** are your terms of payment?
10. A visit ~~of~~ your representative …	10. A visit **by** your representative …
11. ~~We would be appreciated~~ if you …	11. We **would appreciate it** if …
12. Your ~~soon~~ reply would be appreciated.	12. Your **early** reply would be appreciated.
13. We hope to ~~hearing~~ from you soon.	13. We hope to **hear** from you soon.
14. We look forward to ~~hear~~ from you.	14. We look forward to **hearing** from you.

Offers

A | Introduction

Offers are either solicited (sent in response to an enquiry) or unsolicited (sent for marketing purposes on the off-chance that the individual or company may be interested in the goods or services offered). Detailed, specific offers are often called quotations. Offers for work to be carried out, for example, for the redecoration of offices, take the form of cost estimates.

The ability to write an offer is a key skill and is a pre-requisite for the success of a business transaction. It is important to answer enquiries promptly. The offer should be specific and contain all the information necessary for the potential customer to reach a decision. It should include

- details of the products or services offered
- the quantities involved
- prices (+ discounts where applicable)
- terms of payment
- terms of delivery
- times of delivery

In making an offer the seller declares his willingness to sell certain goods or carry out certain services at a certain price and on certain terms.

Offers are binding on the person or company making the offer unless it is expressly stated in the offer that the prices are subject to change without notice or that the offer is either

- without engagement or
- valid until a certain date or
- valid as long as stocks last.

All enquiries should be answered, even if your company does not provide the goods or services required. Where possible recommend an alternative supplier.

B Model correspondence

1 Offer by letter (structure)

HAMMERLIN
Nordwall 45
19055 Schwerin
Tel (+49) 385 77 87 66...
service@hammerlin... .com
www.hammerlin... .com

12 March 201_

Wellbeing Pharmacies
8–12 Hillingdon Road
Hayes
UB4 8TX
England

Your enquiry dated 6 March 201_ `1. subject`

Dear Ms Schwartz `2. personal salutation`

Thank you very much for your interest in our range of medical appliances. Over the last 20 years we have built up a reputation as one of the leading European suppliers of affordable high-precision appliances that are at the cutting edge of the latest technological developments. Our new generation of super-fast glucose-level meters, for instance, is the appliance of choice in many German hospitals where staff esteem their reliability and precision. `3. reference to the enquiry and introduction of the company and its products`

Please refer to our enclosed catalogue and price list for more details on our range of products and services. Prices quoted are EXW Schwerin and our terms of payment are 30% with order, 70 % 30 days after delivery. Delivery can be effected 5 days after receipt of order.
We offer a special 5 % Welcome Discount on the list prices for new customers.
This offer is firm until 15 April 201_. `4. prices, terms of delivery and validity of the offer`

We have recently launched a new series of wristband heart-rate monitors that combine stylish design and the high quality standards that our customers expect from our products. We enclose a sample gift box containing 1 XPC monitor and 4 exchangeable wristbands in dermatologically tested, non-allergic polyvinyl. `5. offer of samples`

If you need further information please contact us at service@hammerlin... .com or talk to one of our customer advisers on (+49) 385 77 87 66... and we will be happy to help you with all your questions. `6. offering further information`

We look forward to receiving your order and trust that you will choose Hammerlin for all your needs in medical technology. `7. goodwill phrase`

Kind regards `8. complimentary close`

Hanna Bauer `9. sender's name and job title`
Export Manager
Encs `10. enclosures`

2 Offer by e-mail

From: sales@abfiltertechnology... .co.uk
To: m.eggensperger@motorenwerke-boeblingen... .com
Date: 4 May 201_
Subject: High-pressure filter unit SF 03

Dear Mr Eggensperger

Many thanks for your enquiry. We are pleased to submit the following quotation for the components requested:

| Items on offer: | 1 unit high-pressure filter unit type SF 03 | Price: GBP 705.00 |
| | 1 unit refill cartridge | Price: GBP 137.00 |

Delivery time: approx. 3 weeks
Terms of delivery: EXW Birmingham
Payment: 30 days net, 10 days 2 per cent
Guarantee period: 12 months for the filter unit
Validity of offer: 3 months
Terms and conditions: subject to our General Terms and Conditions

We hope our offer will prove acceptable to you and look forward to receiving your order.

Best regards
AB Filter Technology

Charlotte Heywood
EU Sales

3 Offer by phone

(ED = Edda Demirel; E = Employee)

ED: Good afternoon. This is Edda Demirel from Barukmoda in Istanbul speaking. Could I speak to Ms Reani Vermeer, please?

E: Good afternoon. I'm afraid, Reani is not in today. Can I take a message for her?

ED: I'm calling about the trial order for 200 pairs of women's winter boots you placed with us some weeks ago. Was everything alright with the consignment?

E: Oh, yes. Everything was fine. The consignment arrived on time and in good condition. We also liked the excellent quality of the leather and the outstanding workmanship .

ED: Oh, I'm really glad to hear that. Have you already heard from your retailers if the boots are selling well?

E: Indeed, they are selling extremely well. Especially the German retailers have run out of stock and are asking for more and similar boots and it's getting very cold here. I was intending to call you myself in the next few days to ask you if we can order more boots at very short notice.

ED: Excellent! So I'm calling at the right time. I'd like to inform you that we are clearing our remaining stocks, as we will need space for our new summer collection soon. Therefore we can grant you a very special discount of 25 % on the list price, if you order a minimum of 300 pairs of boots. It's model PAULA, isn't it? They are still available in all standard sizes. Terms of delivery will remain the same: DAT warehouse Shoeworld in Dieren/ the Netherlands. As to terms of payment they will remain the same as with your last order.

E: That sounds very interesting and I will pass all the information on to Reani when she is back again. I'm sure she will get in touch with you.

ED: But please, tell her this offer is only valid for 10 days.

E: I will. Thank you for calling and good bye.

C | Tool kit

1 Building blocks for business communications: Replies to enquiries/ Making offers

To say thank you for an enquiry

Many thanks Thank you	for	your e-mail enquiring **about** our new selection of … your interest **in** our office furniture.

We refer With reference	to	your phone call regarding … your online enquiry we are pleased to inform you …

To introduce an unsolicited offer

The Bristol Chamber of Commerce has been The Canadian Consulate in Stuttgart has been Ferrars and Brandon Ltd. have been	so kind **as** to give us your address.

May we draw your attention to our special offer for …

To refer to attachments, enclosures or things you are going to send by separate mail

Attached you will find We are pleased to enclose As an attachment we are sending you By separate mail we are sending you	a pdf file several leaflets brochures and price lists our special catalogue	describing for … quoting prices DAT …

To make an offer

We are pleased to quote as follows: …

We would now like to	give you enclose submit	our cost estimate.

We take pleasure in	submitting attaching making	the following quotation **for** …

To state your terms of delivery and payment

Our prices are	quoted to be understood	EXW Chemnitz. FOB Rotterdam. FCA Düsseldorf Airport. CIF Singapore. DAP Birmingham.

We do business on the basis of payment by	sight draft. irrevocable (and confirmed) documentary letter of credit **in** our favour, payable **at** … Bank.

Our usual terms of payment are	cash **with** order. 1/3 **with** order, 1/3 **on** delivery, 1/3 one month after delivery. cash **against** documents. documents **against** acceptance. 30 days net, 10 days 2 %. strictly net **by** the 15th of the month following the month of delivery.

We would request payment by	banker's draft. cheque. bank transfer to our account **with** … Bank.

Regular customers are granted open account terms.

To refer to the delivery time

Delivery Shipment	can be effected will be made	immediately **on** receipt of order. ex stock. two to three weeks after receipt of order.

The delivery period is 6 weeks.

To inform the customer how long the offer is valid

This Our	offer is	valid **until** 7 March. firm until the end of the month. subject to confirmation. without engagement.

The delivery period is 6 weeks.

The offer is subject to prior sale.

To answer specific questions or give additional information

We grant We can offer	20 % quantity discount **for** orders over 10,000 units. a trade discount of 10 % **on/off** our list prices. 2 % cash discount for payment **within** 10 days. 5 % introductory discount.

Please note that	the warranty period is 1 year.
	our prices include assembly on site by our expert engineers.

The	goods articles machinery	are will be	packed transported shipped dispatched sent	in cardboard boxes on pallets. in sturdy wooden crates. in styrofoam-padded cases. in refrigerated containers. **by** air (freight). **by** sea, by vessel. **by** road, by lorry, by rail. **by** courier.

To apologize and explain why you cannot fulfil a request

We regret that Much to our regret Unfortunately	we are unable to supply the … we are not in a position to make you an offer	as we no longer carry this article. because we only sell through our agents. since we are unable to execute the work within the time stipulated in your enquiry.

Please contact one of our distributors in your country, a list of whom is enclosed.

We would suggest that you contact …, who will be able to assist you in this case.

To suggest further contact and encourage further questions

Upon request If you wish	a product presentation could be arranged for. our UK distribution manager could call on you. we could show you the machine in operation at a firm nearby.

Please	call us on +49 202 4670077 send us an e-mail do not hesitate to contact us	should you have any further questions. if you need more detailed information. in case of further queries. if we can assist you any further.

To create goodwill

We hope this quotation will	come up to your expectations. find your approval. meet your requirements.

We look forward to	hearing from you soon. receiving your (trial) order. welcoming you as our customer(s).

We assure you that your order You may rest assured that any order placed	will be	executed carried out dealt with	promptly and carefully.

2 Typical phrases (German/English): Offers

1. Wir danken Ihnen für Ihr Interesse an unseren Spielwaren.	Thank you for your interest in our toys.
2. Als pdf-Datei erhalten Sie unseren neuesten Katalog und unsere Preisliste.	We are sending you our latest catalogue and our price list as a pdf file.
3. Bei Bestellungen von mehr als 1000 Stück gewähren wir 20 % Mengenrabatt.	We grant 20 % quantity discount on orders of more than 1,000 units.
4. Unsere Zahlungsbedingungen lauten: 30 Tage netto, 10 Tage 2 %.	Our terms of payment are: 30 days net, 10 days 2 %.
5. Unsere Preise verstehen sich FCA Flughafen München.	Our prices are to be understood FCA Munich Airport.
6. Zahlung durch unwiderrufliches und bestätigtes Dokumentenakkreditiv zu unseren Gunsten, zahlbar bei der Handels- und Kreditbank Cottbus.	Payment by irrevocable and confirmed documentary letter of credit in our favour, payable at the Handels- und Kreditbank, Cottbus.
7. Wir danken Ihnen für Ihre Anfrage bezüglich Luftfiltern.	Many thanks for your enquiry about air filters.
8. Die Lieferung kann sofort nach Auftragseingang erfolgen.	Delivery can be effected immediately on receipt of order.
9. Wir freuen uns Ihnen mitteilen zu können, dass sämtliche Artikel vorrätig sind.	We are pleased to inform you that all articles are in stock.
10. Leider können wir Ihnen kein Angebot machen, da wir diesen Artikel nicht mehr herstellen.	Unfortunately, we are unable to make you an offer as we no longer manufacture this article.
11. Dieses Angebot ist freibleibend.	The offer is without engagement.
12. Frau Streicher, Nebenstelle 225, erteilt Ihnen gerne weitere Auskünfte.	Frau Streicher will be pleased to give you more information on extension 225.
13. Wir freuen uns Ihnen nachstehendes Angebot unterbreiten zu können.	We are pleased to submit the following offer ...
14. Unsere Lieferzeit beträgt vier bis fünf Wochen.	Our delivery period is four to five weeks.
15. Wir würden uns freuen, einen Probeauftrag von Ihnen zu erhalten.	We would be pleased to get a trial order from you.
16. Wir bitten um Zahlung durch Banküberweisung.	We would ask for payment by bank transfer.
17. Wenn Sie es wünschen, können wir einen Besuch unseres Vertreters veranlassen.	If you so wish, we could arrange for a visit by our representative.
18. Wir versichern Ihnen, dass Ihr Auftrag mit der größten Sorgfalt ausgeführt wird.	We assure you that your order will be executed with the greatest care.
19. Um die Einführung unserer Software auf dem australischen Markt zu erleichtern, gewähren wir 10 % Einführungsrabatt auf unsere Listenpreise.	In order to facilitate the introduction of our software on the Australian market, we will grant 10 % introductory discount on our list prices.
20. Die gewünschten Muster gehen Ihnen mit getrennter Post zu.	The samples requested will be sent to you by separate mail.

D | Avoiding common mistakes

Wrong	Correct
– She has been ~~so kind to~~ give us your name.	– She has been **so kind as to** give us your name.
– Attached you ~~find~~ a pdf file …	– Attached you **will find** a pdf file …
– An offer ~~about~~ …	– An offer **for** …
– We ~~like~~ to make a quotation for …	– We **would like** to make a quotation for …
– Our ~~last~~ catalogue	– Our **latest** catalogue
– We do business on the ~~base~~ of …	– We do business on the **basis** of …
– A letter of credit ~~to~~ our favour …	– A letter of credit **in** our favour …
– Delivery can be ~~affected~~ ex stock.	– Delivery can be **effected** ex stock.
– Payment is to be made ~~until~~ 31 July.	– Payment is to be made **by** 15 July.
– Transport ~~with~~ lorry	– Transport **by** lorry
– We are not in ~~the~~ position to supply …	– We are not in **a** position to supply …
– We ~~suggest to~~ contact …	– We **suggest that** you contact … / We suggest contacting …
– ~~At~~ request	– **On/upon** request
– We look forward to ~~receive~~ your order.	– We look forward to **receiving** your order.

⓪ Useful tips: Offers

– Whenever possible personalise the salutation.
– Thank the enquirer for his interest in your products or services.
– Explicitly or implicitly, e. g. by referring to a price list or to previous business, your offer should contain information on the following points:

1. description of the goods/services offered, e.g. article No, size, colour, features
2. quantity
3. prices and discounts
4. terms of delivery
5. terms of payment
6. delivery period
7. validity of the offer

– Provide all the information requested and any additional information that might be helpful.
– Say something positive about your firm and/or your products.
– Conclude your offer with a phrase designed to make the customer feel positive towards your firm.

Comparing offers and presenting products and statistics

A | Introduction

After receiving various different offers, a company should take a close look and compare them carefully, and not just with regard to price. Other factors also play a decisive role in determining whether an offer is advantageous or not. This includes how favourable the stipulated conditions of payment are and what discounts the various companies offer on different order volumes. The terms of delivery also play a crucial role in determining what the actual end price is going to be. Another point to take into consideration is whether or not the companies can supply when you need the products. Finally, guarantee periods and the provision of after-sales service will be of considerable importance when determining which option to choose.

B | Model offer and model product presentation

1 Offer

⊗ ⊖ ⊕

Dear Ms Ohrt

Thank you for your interest in Texx interactive whiteboards.
We are sending you our latest catalogue as a PDF attachment and are very pleased to give you the details of our quotation:

QTY	ITEM	UNIT PRICE	TOTAL
1	Texx 2007, 70"	€ 2,550.00	€ 2,550.00
2	Texx 2006, 64"	€ 1,960.00	€ 3,920.00
		Total	**€ 6,470.00**

The boards are supplied with integrated loudspeakers and projectors.
All our products carry a two-year warranty and a free replacement service is available.
Our technical helpline is available Mon to Sat between 9 am and 8 pm.
Our prices include delivery. Payment is to be made 14 days after date of invoice.

Please contact me on Derek@customerservice-texx… .aol.com if you have any queries.

Regards
Derek McNeill

Dear Ms Ohrt

Thank you for your interest in our interactive whiteboards. I am happy to attach our latest catalogue and quote you the following prices:

QTY	ITEM	UNIT PRICE	TOTAL
2	**Vectronics XC3** 64" screen, incl. integrated loud-speakers and set-up software	€ 1,230.00	€ 2,460.00
1	**Vectronics TL70** 70" screen, incl. integrated loud-speakers and set-up software	€ 1,880.00	€ 1,880.00
3	**Illumino PJ projectors**	€ 320.00	€ 960.00
			€ 5,300.00

We have a warranty period of 1 year. For delivery charges please consult the last page of the catalogue attached. Please contact me on 0031 10 5564732… if you need any further information.

Yours sincerely
Sofia van Tienen

2 Product presentation

Good morning and welcome to this presentation of the latest range of R4S Security Systems. My name is Joop Snijders and I'd like to give you an overview of our latest products using PowerPoint. I have also brought along some actual, physical products which you can see on the table over there, and which I will later use to demonstrate some special features and functions. I am also going to hand out some leaflets and brochures which give you all the relevant technical details as well as information on prices, warranties, after-sales service and maintenance and much more. After my presentation I will be available to answer any questions and queries that you may have.

Now, let me begin with the latest, improved model of our tried and tested external static CCTV camera "R4S XT". On this first slide you can see that there have been some minor design changes, but overall, it looks very much like the previous model. Like its predecessor it is weatherproof, operates in full colour during normal lighting conditions, but reverts to monochrome when light levels drop.

Let's look at slide two now which reveals a truly fascinating brand new feature. The built-in LED infra-red illumination provides images in complete darkness and has a range of 30 metres. And this is what the images look like. You must admit that the quality is really stunning.

Now, let me just walk over to the table here to show you the real thing. Can everybody see alright? Okay, this tiny contraption here just above the lens …

… Right, this brings us to the end of my presentation which I hope you've enjoyed. Thank you very much for your interest, and now it's over to you, ladies and gentlemen. Are there any questions?

C | Tool kit

1 Phrases: Comparing products

If I had to make a choice I'd	go for pick opt for	the … because	it offers the best value for money. it is cheaper than … of the good customer service.
Yes, I agree, the …	is cheaper than the …,	but the warranty period is shorter.	
As far as	delivery charges are customer service is	concerned	the … is a much better option than the …
All in all, I think the … is the best offer because …			

2 Building blocks for business communications: Presentations

To begin a presentation

My presentation will deal with …

First	I should like to start by telling you …
To begin with	I'd like to introduce …
First of all	I'll focus on …

I intend to keep my presentation as short as possible.

To refer to questions and handouts

I'd welcome any questions at the end of my presentation.

I'll deal with this question later.

Has everyone received a copy of the handout?

To structure the main part of your presentation

My second point is …

Now I should like to	tell you something about …
Next, let me	give you some basic statistics.
Thirdly I'll	move on to …

To emphasize a particular point

The gist of the matter is …	I'd like to illustrate this point by referring to …
An excellent example of this is …	In this connection it is worth mentioning …
Let's look at this issue in particular.	A distinct trend emerges from the following figures …

To conclude your presentation

Finally,	let me say that …
To sum up	I'd like to point out that …
In conclusion	we can see that …

I should like to finish by	thanking the organizers for …
	pointing out that …
	wishing you all …

3 Describing graphs and diagrams

3.1 Line graphs

In line graphs solid (——), broken (- - - - -) or dotted (· · · · · ·) lines serve to represent developments (vertical axis) within a certain period of time (horizontal axis).

The following verbs, nouns, adjectives and adverbs may be used to describe the developments represented in line graphs. Note the prepositions.

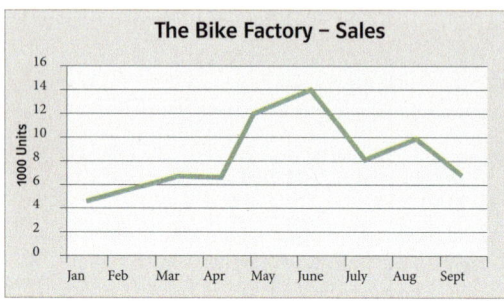

Phrases: Development upwards ↑

to rise/increase/go up/surge /**by** ... **from** ... **to** ...
*In December exports rose **to** around $12 m.*
*Between March and May sales went up **by** 10% **from** 1000 units **to** 1100 units.*

to reach a peak/high/maximum/**of** ...
*In 2013 the price reached a peak **of** $9.25.*

to recover/pick up/rally
Exports recovered in the first quarter.

an increase/a rise/jump/**in** ... **of** ... **to** ...
*There was an increase **in** price **of** 20 % **to** £7,400.*

Phrases: Development downwards ↓

to fall/decline/go down/slump/drop/**by** ... **from** ... **to** ...
*In October sales fell **to** their lowest level.*
*In the course of the second quarter the price declined **by** 2 % **from** $100 **to** $98.*

to reach a low/minimum/**of** ..., to reach a trough/the lowest point/**at** ...
*In the nineties the crime rate reached a low **of** 23,000.*
*In February the lowest point was reached **at** a growth rate of 0.75 per cent.*

a decrease/decline/fall/slowdown/drop/**in** ... **of** ... **to** ...
*In July there was a fall **in** turnover **of** 40 % **to** $780,000.*

Phrases: Development unchanged →

to remain/stay unchanged/stable/flat /**at** ...
*Imports remained unchanged **at** around 120,000 units.*

to fluctuate **between** ... **and** ...
*In recent months prices have been fluctuating **between** $290 **and** $295.*

Phrases: Degree of change

> **Adjectives and adverbs help to describe the speed or degree of the change in movement.**
>
> dramatic(ally)   marked (ly)
> rapid(ly)   steady/steadily
> sudden(ly)   noticeable/noticeably
> steep(ly)   gradual(ly)
> sharp(ly)   moderate(ly)
> substantial(ly)   slow(ly)
> significant (ly)   slight(ly)

3.2 Bar charts

Bar charts are the most effective way of making comparisons, e.g. of a company's imports from different countries, with the help of bars varying in height or length. To describe the comparisons and rankings which are graphically shown in bar charts, use the following expressions:

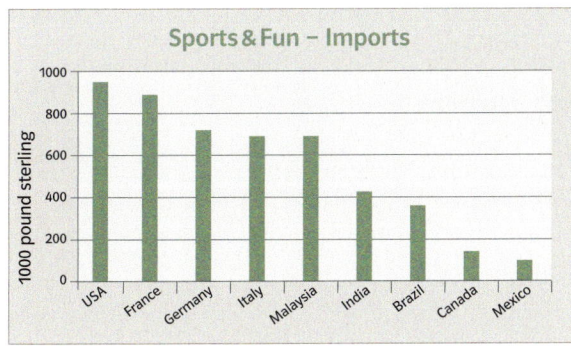

Phrases: Rankings and comparisons

> to be **higher**/lower/bigger/smaller/**more** expensive/**more** developed etc./**than** …
> *Car prices in the UK are **higher than** in Germany.*
>
> to be **as** high/low/big/small/expensive etc./**as** …
> *Earnings are just **as** poor in this industry **as** in the construction industry.*
>
> to be the biggest/smallest/most expensive etc./… **of** …
> *Boots and Belts Ltd is the biggest producer **of** all.*
>
> to be/come first/second/last/next/**with** …
> *Spain comes first **with** 30 m tourists a year.*
>
> to be/follow/**in** first/tenth/last/ place
> *Brighton and Ramsgate are **in** second and third place.*
>
> to be followed **by** …
> *Italy is followed **by** Portugal and Greece, which both import around 350,000 litres per month.*
>
> to be **at** the top/bottom of the list/table/league
> *The USA is **at** the top of the list.*
>
> to bring **up** the rear
> *Germany brings **up** the rear with just 17 per cent.*

3.3 Pie charts

Pie charts are used to show percentages. To describe pie charts you need the following expressions.

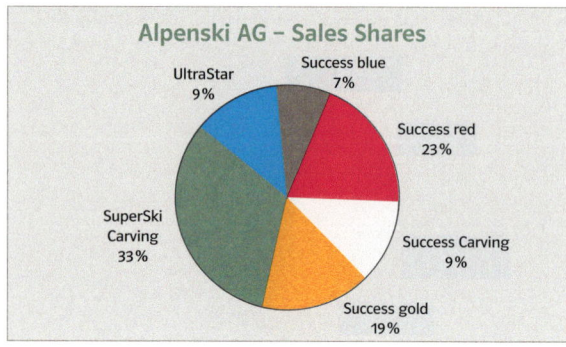

Phrases: shares and percentages

> to make **up** …
> *Nail varnish makes **up** 15 % of the total.*
>
> to account **for** …
> *Lipsticks account **for** three quarters of the turnover of Natural Cosmetics.*
>
> to have a share/percentage/slice **of** …
> *Hairspray has a share **of** only 10 per cent.*

4 Typical phrases (German/English): Presentations

1. Meine Präsentation behandelt die Entwicklung auf dem indischen Markt.	My presentation will deal with the development on the Indian market.
2. Als Erstes möchte ich Ihnen unsere Firma vorstellen.	First I should like to introduce our company.
3. Ich möchte meine Präsentation so kurz wie möglich halten.	I intend to keep my presentation as short as possible.
4. Mein zweiter Punkt ist die Entwicklung in Wales.	My second point is the development in Wales.
5. Zunächst werde ich mich auf die Verkaufszahlen des letzten Jahres konzentrieren.	To begin with I'll focus on last year's sales figures.
6. Auf diese Frage werde ich später zurückkommen.	I'll return to this question later.
7. Haben Sie alle ein Exemplar des Handzettels bekommen?	Has everyone received a copy of the handout?
8. Ich wäre gerne bereit, etwaige Fragen an Schluss meiner Präsentation zu beantworten.	I'd welcome any questions at the end of my presentation.

9. In diesem Zusammenhang sollte man die Lage in China erwähnen.	In this connection the situation in China is worth mentioning.
10. Ein hervorragendes Beispiel dafür ist das Wachstum des Exports.	An excellent example of this is the growth in exports.
11. Zusammenfassend können wir erkennen, dass unsere Strategie erfolgreich war.	In conclusion we can see that our strategy has been successful.
12. Nun möchte ich Ihnen etwas zu Artikel 217 sagen.	Now I'd like to tell you something about article 217.
13. Aus folgenden Zahlen ergibt sich ein deutlicher Trend.	A distinct trend emerges from the following figures.
14. Als Nächstes lassen Sie mich Ihnen ein paar grundlegende Statistiken vorlegen.	Next, let me give you some basic statistics.
15. Abschließend möchte ich den Organisatoren der Konferenz danken.	I should like to finish by thanking the organisers of the conference.
16. Als Drittes möchte ich zu den Reisekosten übergehen.	Thirdly, I'd like to move on to travelling expenses.
17. Dieses Problem wollen wir uns vor allem ansehen.	Let's look at this issue in particular.

> ⓘ **INFO: Graphs and tenses**
>
> Past developments are described using the simple past (In January prices fell by 17%.). When the period of time described is not completed, the present perfect must be used (This year we have so far seen a marked increase in sales.).
> What is going on at present should be described using the present continuous (Prices are fluctuating at the moment). Whenever a graph becomes a projection into the future, the will-future or another appropriate verb form must be used for the description (During the next few months prices are expected to rise to last year's levels.).

Orders

A | Introduction

1 Legal aspects

Under **German law** an order placed in reply to a firm offer results in a contract. Accordingly, the seller must deliver the goods at the place agreed upon within the period agreed upon, whereas the buyer must accept the goods and pay the price agreed upon within the period agreed upon.

Under **English[1] law** the following essential elements are required for the creation of a **legal contract**:

(a) Offer and acceptance.
There must be an offer by one party (the offeror) and an acceptance of it by the other (the offeree). The contract comes into existence when an offer has been unconditionally accepted. The acceptance may be made orally, in writing or by conduct.

(b) Consideration.
Consideration may be in the form of a payment of money, a delivery of goods, a performance of services or promises to do or make any of these.

(c) Intention to create legal relations.
In business relations the law will presume that the parties entering into agreement intend those agreements to have legal consequences.
A **contract of sale** is a specific type of legal contract whereby goods, services or property are to be exchanged from seller (or vendor) to buyer (or purchaser) for an agreed upon value of money or the promise to pay same.
Much of the English law governing the sale of goods is codified in the Sale of Goods Act 1979, which was amended by the Sale and Supply of Goods Act 1994.

[1] **"British" law** does not exist as Scotland has a legal system of its own. The legal systems of Wales and Northern Ireland also differ from English law to some extent.

2 Commercial aspects

A **trial order** is placed for a small quantity to test the merchandise or service. **Repeat orders** cover the goods or services ordered previously. **Standing orders** ensure that identical quantities are supplied at regular intervals. **Orders on call**, i.e. orders placed for large quantities called for at irregular intervals, play an important role within the concept of just-in-time delivery.

Nowadays many orders in **B2B (business to business) transactions** are placed online. After registering with the supplier, a company may place orders via the supplier's website. Firms that regularly do business with each other have immediate access to their partners' IT systems.

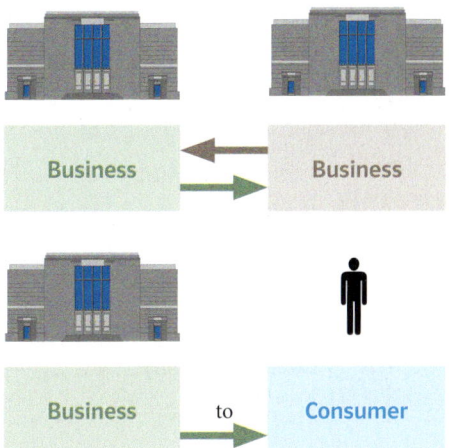

In **B2C (business to consumer) transactions** this method is also widely used. In this case payment is often made by credit card and the customer is required to reveal the number and expiry date of his credit card. Since some people regard this procedure as somewhat risky, regular customers can be given a PIN (personal identification number) and need not indicate credit card details with purchases they make online. The amount due is debited against their bank account.

Special forms are often used for ordering goods or services. The customer may use his own or one provided by the seller. The forms are usually called "purchase order" or order form. If a form is not available you should make sure that you provide all the essential information. Failure to provide accurate and complete information may result in delays or cause misunderstandings. Use the following checklist:

- ☑ date and order number
- ☑ item number (catalogue number, article number, model number, etc.)
- ☑ quantity desired (often in large units such as dozens, cases, etc.)
- ☑ name of the item being ordered
- ☑ description (size, colour, extra features, etc.)
- ☑ unit price
- ☑ discounts
- ☑ total amount
- ☑ terms of payment and delivery
- ☑ delivery address
- ☑ delivery time/date
- ☑ signature

B | Model orders

1 Model letter and order form

Rupert & Gateby
Wiesbadener Landstr. 244
60889 Frankfurt
Germany

R4S Security Systems
Julianalaan 233
1118 CP Schiphol
Netherlands

28 March 201_

Order No. 7864

Dear Mr Snijders

Thank you very much for your quotation of 15 March 201_.

I am very pleased to inform you that Rupert & Gateby have decided to place an order for the items specified on the form enclosed.

We would be grateful if you could arrange for delivery and installation of the equipment to be carried out in CW 15 – preferably on the Wednesday or Thursday. Please let me know what day/time would be most convenient for you.

We would also appreciate it if you could let us have a brief confirmation of receipt of this order.

I look forward to hearing from you soon.

Kind regards

Annika Borawski
Annika Borawski
Premises Manager

ORDER FORM		**R4S** Security Systems BV			**7864**
CODE	ITEM	QTY	UNIT PRICE €	AMOUNT €	
R4S XT	External static CCTV camera	2	588.00	1,176.00	
R4S DC	Internal dome CCTV camera	4	325.00	1,300.00	
TL	Biometric reader system	1	659.00	659.00	
	Total incl. delivery and instalment			3,135.00	
SIGNATURE:			DATE:		

2 Structure of a detailed order

⊗ ⊖ ⊕

From: k.hauptmann@reisewelt... .de
To: croft@northeastluggage... .co.uk
Date: 19 Feb 201_
Subject: Your offer for Crinkle Nylon Trolleys   `1. subject line`
Attachments: Purchase Order no. GB/245

Dear Mr Croft   `2. personal salutation`

Thank you very much for your e-mail offer of 14 March.   `3. reference to offer`

As an attachment we are sending you our Purchase Order no. GB/245 for a total of 150 Crinkle Nylon Trolleys. `4. order (quantity, description, etc.)`

We would like to confirm that the price per unit is €69.50 less 5% quantity discount.   `5. prices and discounts`

Payment will be made by bank transfer on receipt of invoice.   `6. terms of payment`

Delivery is to be effected CIP Finsterwalde.   `7. terms of delivery`

The goods must reach us by 15 May at the latest, and we reserve the right to cancel the order after that date.   `8. delivery time`

The goods are to be delivered to our warehouse at Berliner Chaussee 83, 03238 Finsterwalde. Please instruct your forwarders accordingly.   `9. instructions, if necessary`

If this order is executed to our full satisfaction, you may expect further substantial orders from us.   `10. appropriate ending`

Regards   `11. complimentary close`
Karola Hauptmann
Reisewelt Finsterwalde

C | Tool kit

1 Building blocks for business communications: Orders

To refer to previous contacts and place an order

We have received	your quotation		would now like to order the following items:
We thank you for	your offer	and	are pleased to attach our Purchase Order no. …
We have studied	your brochure		would ask you to supply …

We herewith confirm the order we placed by telephone as follows:

	deliver		items		terms	given	in your offer.
Please	send us	the following	goods	on the		stated	below.
	supply		articles		conditions	mentioned	in your catalogue.

Thank you for your cost estimate for the repairs.

To specify articles and prices

Quantity	Article No.	Description	Colour	Unit price	Total
50	400-03	Arch Spotlight	chrome-plated	€ 12.50	€ 625.00
30	400-07	Wave Spotlight	satin nickel finish	€ 13.50	€ 405.00

To confirm prices and discounts

We wish to place an order **for** model AC/7	**at** the price **of** priced **at**	€ 115.00, less 5 %	quantity discount. introductory discount. trade discount.

We would like to confirm that the prices are	taken **from** your current price list. as follows: … as per your price list **of** 1 September.

We are pleased to note that you will grant us an initial order discount **of** 3% **on** your list prices.

To confirm the date, method and terms of payment

As agreed As requested	we will make payment	**on** receipt of the goods. **within** 10 days after date **of** invoice. **by** bank transfer **to** your account **with** ABC bank. **by** cheque/**by** banker's draft.

Payment will be	made effected	**by** irrevocable and confirmed letter of credit, to be opened **in** your favour, payable **at** a major London bank and valid **until** 31 March. **by** bill of exchange 60 days **after** sight. **on** the basis of documents against payment. one third **with** order, one third **on** delivery , one third 30 days **after** delivery.

To confirm terms of delivery

As agreed, delivery will be made DAP Leipzig.

Your above-mentioned prices The prices mentioned in your offer	are quoted CIF Mumbai. are to be understood FCA Munich airport.

To confirm the delivery date and specify qualifications

Please note that	we expect delivery to be made the goods must be dispatched the goods ordered must arrive	**at** the beginning of May. as soon as possible. **in** the course of week 38. **within** the next 24 hours. **by** 1 November at the latest.

We would ask you to confirm that the goods can be delivered **from** stock.

We regret we will have We will be obliged We reserve the right	to cancel our order	if the consignment is delivered late. if the goods do not reach us within two weeks. if the delivery period is not observed.

Delivery by the date stipulated in the sales contract is a firm condition of this order.

To give instructions

Please	ensure make sure arrange	that	the sets are the articles are the merchandise is	not exposed to heat during transport. sent by courier. transported by air. insured against all risks. packed with the utmost care.

We would appreciate **it** if the consultant could send us his manuscript two weeks in advance.

To close the communication

We look forward **to**	your acknowledgement of our order. receiving the goods in due time. taking delivery of our order as soon as possible. placing further orders with your firm.

Thank you for your prompt attention to this order.

2 Typical phrases (German/English): Orders

	German	English
1.	Wir haben Ihr Angebot vom 23. März erhalten und freuen uns, unsere Bestellung Nr. GB/18a anhängen zu können.	We have received your quotation of 23 March and are pleased to attach our Purchase Order No. GB/18a.
2.	Wie gewünscht erfolgt die Zahlung per Banküberweisung auf Ihr Konto bei der Merchant Bank.	As requested, payment will be made by bank transfer to your account with Merchant Bank.
3.	Bitte nehmen Sie zur Kenntnis, dass die Lieferung eine Woche vor Weihnachten erfolgen muss.	Please note that delivery must be effected one week before Christmas.
4.	Falls die Lieferfrist nicht eingehalten wird, werden wir gezwungen sein, den Auftrag zu stornieren.	We will be obliged to cancel the order if the delivery period is not observed.
5.	Wir sehen dem Erhalt der Ware entgegen und freuen uns auf weitere Geschäfte mit Ihnen.	We look forward to receiving the goods and to doing further business with you.
6.	Wir bestätigen hiermit unseren telefonisch erteilten Auftrag wie folgt:	We herewith confirm the order we placed by telephone as follows:
7.	Hiermit bestellen wir 200 Brieftaschen aus Leder, Art.-Nr. W75-a, schwarz, zu einem Stückpreis von £ 27.90, Gesamtwert £ 5580,00.	We would like to order 200 leather wallets, article No. W75-a, black, at a unit price of £27.90, total value £5,580.00.
8.	Bitte stellen Sie sicher, dass die Teile per Kurier geschickt werden und im Laufe des Tages hier eintreffen.	Please make sure that the components are sent by courier and reach us in the course of today.
9.	Wir möchten Sie bitten, uns die bestellten Kaffeebecher CIP Wiesbaden zu senden.	We would ask you to send us the coffee mugs ordered CIP Wiesbaden.
10.	Bitte bestätigen Sie, dass die Ware ab Lager geliefert werden kann.	Please confirm that the goods can be delivered from stock.

11. Bitte sorgen Sie dafür, dass die Teetassen äußerst sorgfältig verpackt werden.	Please see to it that the tea cups are packed with the utmost care.
12. Die Zahlungsbedingungen lauten: Unwiderrufliches und bestätigtes Akkreditiv zu Ihren Gunsten, zahlbar bei einer Londoner Großbank, gültig bis 31. Juli 201_.	The terms of payment are: by irrevocable and confirmed letter of credit in your favour, payable at a major London bank, valid until 31 July 201_.
13. Die Preise sind Ihrer neuesten Preisliste entnommen und verstehen sich EXW Glasgow.	The prices have been taken from your current price list and are to be understood EXW Glasgow.
14. Wir bitten Sie, uns 700 Stück zu den nachfolgend genannten Bedingungen zu liefern.	We would ask you to supply 700 units on the conditions mentioned below.
15. Wir freuen uns, dass Sie sich bereit erklärt haben, uns einen Einführungsrabatt von 20 % zu gewähren.	We are pleased to note that you are prepared to grant us an introductory discount of 20 %.

D | Avoiding common mistakes

Wrong	Correct
– Please ~~supply us article~~ no. 350.	– Please **supply article** No. 350/
	– Please **supply us with article** No. 350
– … ~~to~~ the terms stated in your offer.	– … **on** the terms stated in your offer.
– We would like to place an order ~~about~~ …	– We would like to place an order **for** …
– … ~~to~~ the price of Euro 17.50.	– … **at** the price of Euro 17.50.
– … ~~minus~~ 30 % trade discount.	– … **less** 30% trade discount.
– Prices are taken ~~out of~~ your ~~actual~~ price list.	– Prices are taken **from** your **current** price list.
– Payment ~~is effected~~ on receipt of the goods.	– Payment **will be effected** on receipt of the goods.
– Payment will be made ~~with~~ cheque.	– Payment will be made **by** cheque.
– … by letter of credit, payable ~~by~~ a London bank.	– … by letter of credit, payable **with** a London bank.
– … one third ~~on~~ order, one third ~~by~~ delivery	– … one third **with** order, one third **on** delivery
– Delivery must be made ~~in~~ the beginning of May.	– Delivery must be made **at** the beginning of May.
– The ~~ordered goods~~ must reach us …	– The **goods ordered** must reach us …
– We would ~~appreciate if~~ …	– We would **appreciate it if** …
– Please ~~care for~~ immediate delivery.	– Please **arrange for** immediate delivery.
	– Please **ensure** that delivery is effected immediately.
– We look forward to ~~place~~ further orders with you.	– We look forward to **placing** further orders with you.

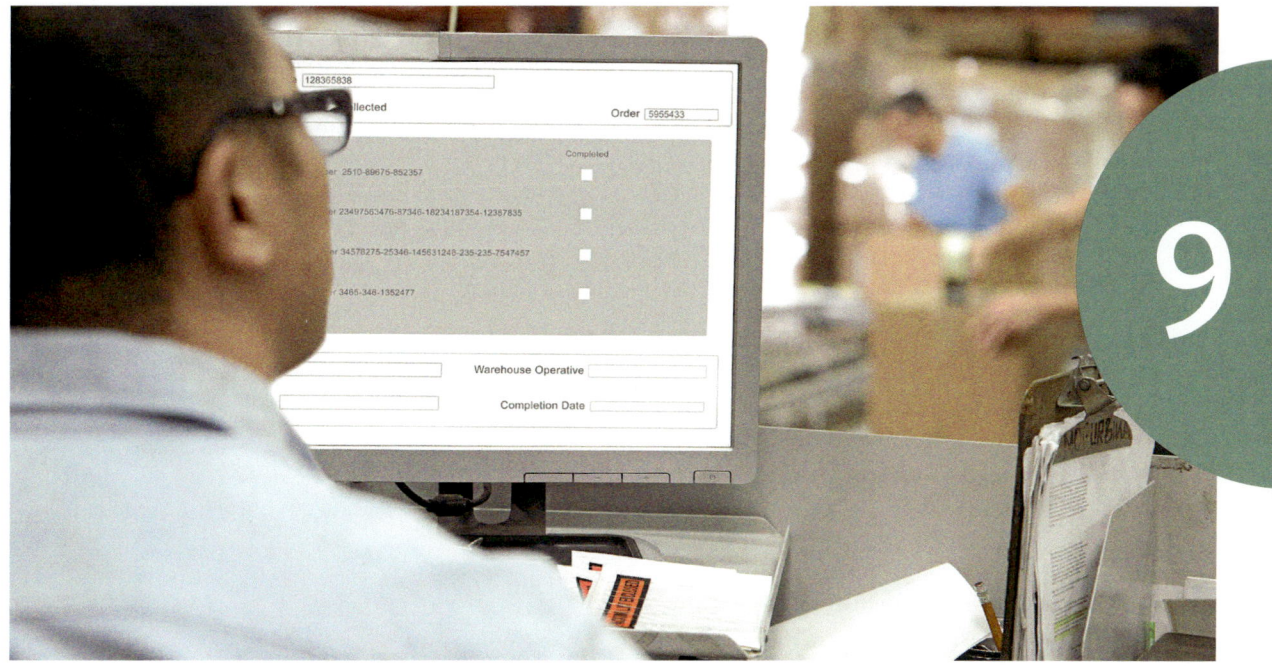

9

Order confirmation and cancellation

A | Introduction

Nowadays orders are often no longer acknowledged, especially if the order is to be executed straight away. However, orders placed by telephone, e-mail or via a company website are confirmed by e-mail. Some companies immediately send an invoice on receipt of the order, which acts as confirmation. Confirming an order reduces uncertainty and is a service that lets the customer know that their order has been received and is being dealt with. This helps to build goodwill.

First orders should be confirmed as they present an opportunity of welcoming the new customer and establishing a new business relationship. The confirmation of an order from an established customer is also a sign of appreciation and signals that orders are not simply taken for granted. Orders placed on the basis of an offer without engagement or an offer with some reservation, for instance regarding prices or quantities available, must in any case be confirmed by the supplier for a contract to come into being.

The order confirmation should let the customer know that the order is being dealt with and should contain the following information:
– date and number of the order
– details of goods ordered
– reference to the invoice
– date and method of dispatch
– terms of payment and delivery

It may also be a good idea to enclose information/brochures about other products which may be of interest to the customer and thus generate further orders.

Sometimes the confirmation of order contains particulars of the impending or effected dispatch of the goods. In some instances a separate advice of dispatch may have to be sent to the customer.

B | Model letters

1 Cancellation of order by letter

Rupert & Gateby
Wiesbadener Landstr. 244
60889 Frankfurt
Germany

R4S Security Systems
Julianalaan 233
1118 CP Schiphol
Netherlands

3 April 201_

Order No. 7864 / 28 March 201_

Dear Mr Snijders,

I am very sorry to inform you that Rubert & Gateby have no alternative but to ask you to cancel the above order. I do realise that this is very short notice as you have already confirmed our order and informed me last week that the items are ready to be despatched and installed by your team in CW 14.

You will be aware of the devastating storms and subsequent flooding that affected the Greater Frankfurt area last week. As a result, our premises have been severely affected.

I am sure you will appreciate that this is causing major disruption to our operations and it will take some time to assess the exact extent of the damage before we are able to return to normal.

Once damage assessment has been carried out and repair works are under way I will contact you again to discuss how best to proceed with our order.

In the meantime, please accept my sincere apologies for any inconvenience this may cause to your business.

Kind regards

Annika Borawski
Annika Borawski
Premises Manager

2 Order confirmation by e-mail

To:
From:

Dear Ms Knowles,

Thank you very much for your order No. 89/9921 which we received this morning.

As agreed, the items listed below will be despatched as soon as we receive your payment.

15 scanning pens THD 65 – unit price € 23.95
Installation software (CD-ROM/USB-stick) – € 6.05

Delivery will be made by Red Arrow Parcel Service to the address provided in your order.

Red Arrow will send you a text message on the day of delivery to let you know what time the courier will arrive.

If you have any further queries regarding your order please do not hesitate to contact me any time between 9am and 5pm, Mon to Fri on 0049 2328 795 6782. Alternatively, visit our website at www.elektronikon... .de/customerservice/myorders and type in your order number to view the status of your order.

We look forward to being at your service again in the near future.

Best regards

Oliver Schmaltz
Sales Department
elektronikon GmbH

3 Informal confirmation by e-mail

To:
From:

Hello Mr Schneider,

Thanks for your time today.
This is to confirm that I have booked £342 + VAT for a position on our What's On newsletter in the Bristol area.

Ad Ref: salespage.fridayad... .co.uk/FridayAd

This has been paid by debit card ending ...7940 by yourself over the telephone.

I will design your advert with the copy around your last paper advert as agreed by yourself and link this to your website for 6 weeks.

I will send a copy of the newsletter out to your email.

Kind Regards
Alison Broker | Online Media Sales Executive
Weekend Ad Ltd | 0807 106 23702... Ext: 6255

C | Tool kit

1 Building blocks for business communications: Confirmation and cancellation of orders

To refer to the order

Thank you for	your order No. RF/62	of	23 May,
We have received		dated	

To confirm the order

which we now	confirm	as follows:
	acknowledge	

We are pleased to	confirm	your order **for** USB sticks.
We herewith	acknowledge	

Our order confirmation is attached.

To refer to particulars of your offer

As stated in our offer	our prices are quoted for delivery CPT Sunderland.
As agreed	

We are pleased to confirm that you will be granted a quantity discount of 15%.

To say what you have done or are going to do about the delivery

We have instructed	our forwarders	to arrange for prompt delivery.
	the haulage company XYZ	to collect the goods at our warehouse.
	our shipping agents	to have the goods transported by air.

As arranged	the consignment will be	dispatched	by refrigerated lorry.
As requested	the goods will be	shipped	by air freight.
	the order will be	delivered	by train.
		forwarded to you	by courier.
		sent	as a part container load.

The articles	are expected to arrive	**on** or **about** 23 March.
The boxes	are due to reach you	**by** the middle of next month.
The goods		**within** two weeks.
		next Tuesday.

To acknowledge instructions

Your instructions	concerning	packing	will be strictly	observed.
	as to	documentation		adhered to.
	regarding	just-in-time delivery		

To close the letter

Thank you for placing this order **with** us. We assure you that it will be	given priority. dealt with promptly and carefully. executed with the greatest care.

We assure you that the delivery deadline **of** 31 July will be met without fail.

Delivery will be effected **by** Friday, 30 October, at the latest.

We are confident that the cameras will **come up to** your expectations.

We look forward to	doing further business with you. serving you again.

To refuse an order

Much as we should like to do business with you, we fear that we cannot economically manufacture such small quantities.

As we only sell **through** our agents Since we only supply to authorised dealers As wholesalers supplying to retailers only	we have no alternative **but** to decline the order.

We regret that as a result of the shortage of skilled programmers we are unable to accept your order.

To apologise and suggest alternatives

We regret to inform you that We are sorry that Unfortunately,	the model you ordered is the goods in question are articles 470 and 472 are	no longer produced by us. no longer available in Germany. temporarily **out of stock**.

However, we could	offer you supply	article 471 a very similar model	**from** stock. as a substitute.

To cancel an order

We	are very sorry but we must deeply regret having to are much to our regret compelled to	cancel our order	due to owing to as a result of	an unexpected tightening of import regulations. the sudden insolvency of our customer. the severe recession following the earthquake.

We hope We assure you	that we will soon be able	to place to give you to make up for the loss by placing	another order.

2 An order form

FIRST NAME			SURNAME		DELIVER TO	
Address					Address	
POSTCODE					POSTCODE	
QTY	ITEM		VINTAGE		PRICE PER BOTTLE	TOTAL
					TOTAL	
DATE OF ORDER					DATE OF DISPATCH	

D | Avoiding common mistakes

Wrong	Correct
1. Thank you for your order ~~from~~ 23 May.	1. Thank you for your order **of/dated** 23 May.
2. We confirm your order ~~of~~ handbags.	2. We confirm your order **for** handbags.
3. The goods will arrive ~~at~~ 18 August.	3. The goods will arrive **on** 18 August.
4. The articles will be shipped ~~until~~ Friday at the latest.	4. The articles will be shipped **by** Friday at the latest.
5. Please ~~let~~ the machine ~~be transported~~ by sea.	5. Please **have** the machine **transported** by sea.
6. Delivery will be ~~affected~~ by 31 July.	6. Delivery will **be effected** by 31 July.
7. Your instructions will be ~~exactly kept~~.	7. Your instructions will be **strictly adhered to**.
8. We hope the goods will ~~correspond to~~ your expectations.	8. We hope the goods will **come up to** your expectations.
9. We have no alternative ~~than~~ to decline your order.	9. We have no alternative **but** to decline your order.
10. We should like to ~~make~~ further business with you.	10. We should like **to do** further business with you.

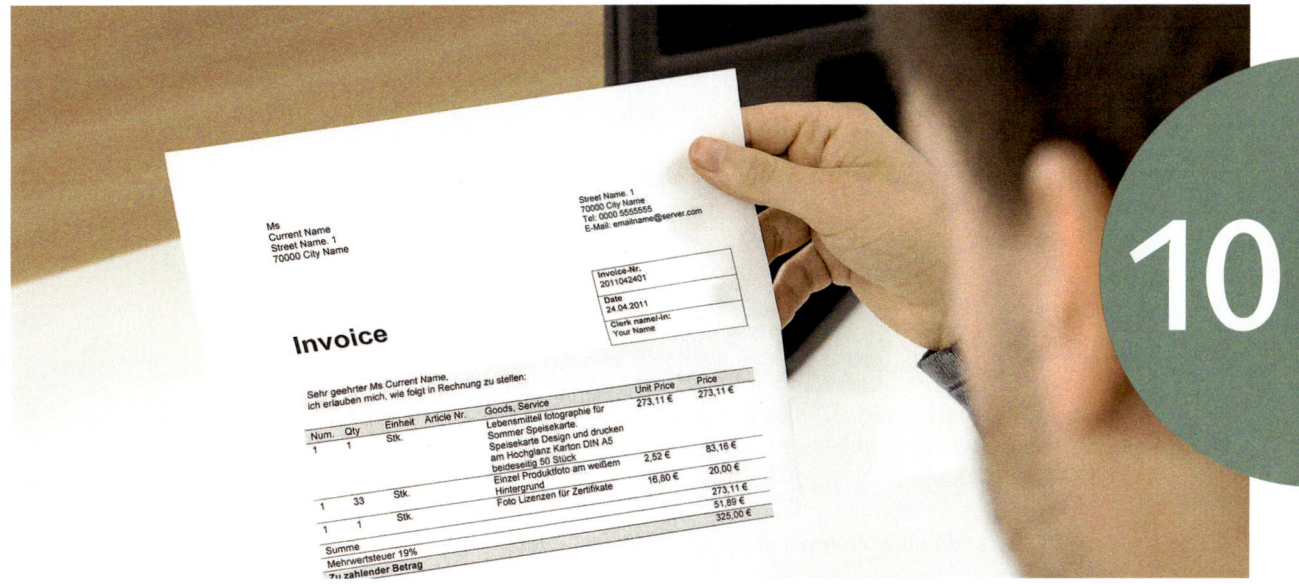

Payment

A | Introduction

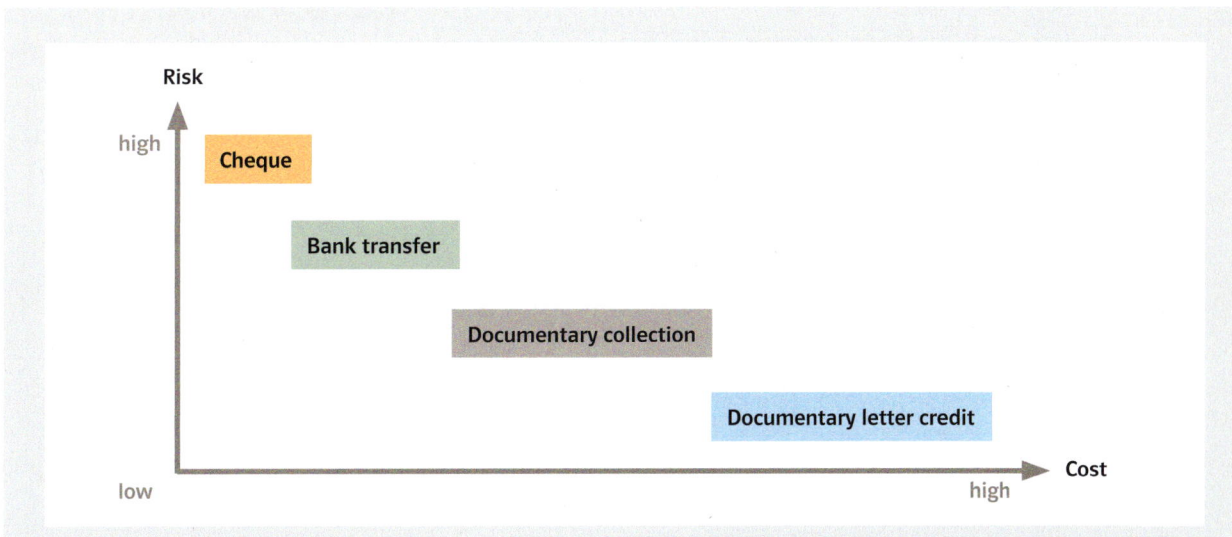

Payment can be effected by

– Bank transfer
– Cheque
– Banker's draft
5 – Letter of credit
– Bill of exchange
– Credit card and debit card

Credit cards are issued by credit card companies in order to give their customers credit when they 10 purchase goods or services. When the cardholder buys something he or she presents the credit card to the salesperson and signs a transaction slip. The amount in question is advanced by the credit card company and the cardholder normally gets a 15 monthly statement of account to be paid in full or by instalments. Some credit card companies charge annual fees. The advantages of credit cards are convenience and relative security.

A **debit (or charge) card** is issued by a bank. The account-holder may use it to pay for goods and services in shops without handling cash. It differs from a credit card in that the customer's account is immediately debited with the amount of the transaction. Debit cards can also be used to withdraw money from cash points (ATMs). The German EC card is a debit card. Debit cards do not exist in the USA.

1 Terms of payment in international trade

The terms of payment chosen in an international transaction will depend on the size of the order, the creditworthiness of the customer and the banking system and political situation in the customer's country. The following examples of terms are listed roughly in the order of the degree of security provided for the seller.

LOW

1. **Cash with order** (CWO): The seller demands that cash covering the cost of merchandise and delivery accompany the customer's order.

2. **Payment in advance**: Similar to CWO. Payment must be effected before shipment. It provides maximum security for the seller, e.g. when the goods have to be manufactured to buyer's specifications.

3. **Letter of Credit** (see page 168)

4. **Documents against payment** (D/P) (see page 171)

5. **Cash on delivery** (COD): The carrier (e.g. the postman) will hand over the goods to the buyer against payment or against written proof by the bank that payment has been effected.

6. **Payment on receipt of invoice**: Payment becomes due when the invoice is received.

RISK

7. **Staggered payment**: Payment is spread over a period of time, e.g. "One third with order, one third on delivery, one third 30 days after delivery." Such terms are customary with large orders involving the supply of goods, such as machinery, and the provision of services such as installation and start-up of the equipment.

8. **Open credit**: The seller grants the buyer credit by stipulating terms like "30 days net, 10 days 2 %", which means that the buyer has to remit the full invoice amount within 30 days. If he pays the amount within 10 days he will be entitled to deduct 2 % cash discount from the invoice amount. Open credit terms provide little security for the seller but are widely used in transactions involving comparatively small sums and/or trusted customers.

HIGH

9. **Documents against acceptance** (D/A) (see page 171)

10. **Bill of Exchange** (B/E) at e.g. 60 days (see Unit 7)

11. **Open account terms** (see next page)

> ⓘ **INFO**
>
> The words 'terms net' on an invoice mean no discount is allowed. The words 'prompt settlement' mean no credit period is allowed.

2 Open account terms

Open account terms are typically granted to well-established and trusted customers. An open account transaction is one where the goods are shipped and delivered before
5 payment is due. The buyer/importer does not settle individual invoices but waits for the statement of account which is generally sent out on a fixed date each month or every quarter and shows the balance outstanding on
10 the customer's account. After he has received the statement the customer pays for the goods according to the terms agreed, e.g. 10 days 2 %, 30 days net.

Open account terms are obviously advantag-
15 eous for the buyer as the seller effectively grants him credit. This may be an important factor in securing sales and gaining an edge over competitors. However, it is also risky for the seller and should only be extended where
20 the buyer is reliable and creditworthy. In longstanding, regular business relations it is customary to trade on 'open account terms'.

The statement of account is a business document which shows the balance
25 outstanding on a buyer's account and requests payment. Smaller firms usually send out statements on the last day of the month, while large companies spread out billing over the entire month. Thus, some customers get their
30 statements on the 10th of each month while others get their statements on the 20th, etc.

3 Letter of credit

There are a number of risks involved in inter-national trade which are greater than in the domestic market. The exporter may not get paid. This would be a considerable loss given
5 the costs of manufacturing and shipping the goods abroad. The risk for the importer is that he may never receive the goods if he pays in advance. Obviously, it is necessary to find some arrangement that addresses the concerns of
10 both parties.

The letter of credit, in foreign trade also called **documentary credit**, provides security for both buyer and seller and has consequently become one of the most widely used methods of pay-
15 ment, involving four parties: the exporter and his bank, and the importer and his bank. It is an undertaking by the importer's bank, the **opening bank**, to pay a certain sum to the exporter upon presentation of specified
20 documents. Consequently, it is not just the importer who is obliged to pay. In addition, the exporter can rely on the promise to pay made by the importer's bank. In the case of a **con-firmed** letter of credit a second bank, this time
25 the **advising bank** in the exporter's country, also assumes responsibility for payment under the letter of credit.

Nowadays letters of credit are almost always **irrevocable**, that is to say they can only be
30 revoked with the consent of all the parties involved. Frequently, the shipping documents to be presented by the exporter are accompa-nied by a sight draft or time bill drawn by the exporter on the importer or his bank.

The basic procedure is as follows:

1. Importer and exporter negotiate the terms of the transaction.
    The importer agrees to payment by letter of credit (L/C).

2. The importer instructs his bank to open a letter of credit in favour of the exporter.

3. The importer's bank (the opening bank) issues an irrevocable letter of credit and informs the exporter's bank (also known as the advising bank) and confirms the letter of credit if a confirmed L/C was agreed on in the sales contract.

4. The exporter is notified that the letter of credit has been opened in his favour.

5. The exporter ships the goods as specified in the L/C and receives the Bill of Lading which is a document of title and confers ownership of the goods.

6. The exporter presents the required documents (including the Bill of Lading) to his bank.

7. The exporter's bank checks that the documents conform to the specifications of the L/C and pays the exporter (assuming that the L/C has been confirmed by his bank).

8. The exporter's bank sends the documents to the importer's bank, which also checks them.

9. The importer's bank pays either the exporter the amount of the L/C or, if it is a confirmed L/C, the exporter's bank.

10. The importer's bank releases the documents to the importer and debits his account.

11. The importer can now take possession of the goods as he now has the Bill of Lading, which confers ownership of the goods.

B | Model fax

DIY-HEAVEN

2877 Pleasanton Rd | San Antonio | TX 78112 | USA | Fax: +1 210 677 895 22 . . .

TELEFAX MESSAGE

Blauhelm AG, Am Freihafen 34, 20883 Hamburg, Germany

Attn.: Helmut Hubschmied	**Fax: 0049 40 759 309 10 . . .**
From: Dawn Shaeffer	**sent: 201__/04/30 09:56**

Re: Your order confirmation of 201__/04/29; order No. BM-87-455

Dear Helmut:

Thank you very much for your order confirmation and pro-forma invoice that we received yesterday.

I am very pleased to inform you that we have instructed our bank to issue an irrevocable letter of credit in your favor.

The L/C will be available thru Hansebank Hamburg who will inform you of the type and number of documents required for this transaction.

We look forward to receiving your shipment.

Cordially

Dawn Shaeffer
Dawn Shaeffer
Purchase Manager

C | Tool kit

1 Building blocks for business communications: Payment

To refer to the invoice or statement of account

We are enclosing	• our pro forma invoice as requested.
	• our quarterly statement of account showing a balance of £437.50 in our favour.
	• invoice no … amounting to US$ … and would appreciate early settlement.

To announce payment

We have instructed our bank to remit the invoice amount to your account **with** … Bank.			

We are sending you enclosed our cheque	in part payment	of your invoice no …
	in full settlement	
	as the first instalment **under** our agreement.	

To refer to discrepancies

When checking your invoice Comparing the statement with our own records	we noticed the following	error. omission. discrepancies.

It seems that you	forgot to deduct the quantity discount. made an error in totalling. omitted the amount of the credit note.

Please let us have a credit note for the difference.

To ask for more favourable terms of payment

As we have now been doing business on the basis of	documents against payment cash on delivery payment on receipt of invoice	**for** two years **since** last May	we would like to ask you to grant us open account terms.

To refer to bills of exchange

As arranged we have drawn **on** you	**at** 60 days' sight. **for** £1200.00 payable at sight. a B/E at 90 days.

We are herewith returning your draft provided with our acceptance and will duly honour the bill **at** maturity.

The documents will be surrendered to you by the bank against	payment of the sight draft. acceptance of the bill of exchange.

To refer to payment by letter of credit

Payment is to be	made effected	**by** irrevocable (and confirmed) letter **of** credit **in** our favour, payable **at** a German bank and valid **until** 31 July.

We will instruct We have asked	our bank to	open a series of monthly irrevocable letters of credit **of** US$ 21,730 each, **in** your favour. issue an irrevocable letter of credit **in** your favour, valid **until** …

The L/C	is to be confirmed by will be available through	Varanasi Merchant Bank, Mumbai.

The letter of credit will be available against presentation of the following documents:

Please submit the following documents: Please note that the following documents must be presented:	commericial invoice bill of lading air waybill consignment note insurance certificate certificate of origin packing list inspection certificate	in duplicate. in triplicate. in quadruplicate. 3-fold.

Documents required:	• full set of clean on board bill of lading • insurance policy covering all risks • certificate of analysis

Your bank will advise you of the kind and number of documents required.

Terms forming part of an L/C:	• latest date of shipment 30 September • expiry date 29 March • partial shipments allowed • transshipment not allowed

2 Typical phrases (German/English): Payment

1.	Wir fügen unsere Rechnung Nr. 328 über €42 764,50 bei und bitten Sie, diesen Betrag auf unser Konto … bei der Stadtsparkasse Wuppertal zu überweisen.	In the attachment we are sending you our Invoice No. 328 for €42,764.50 and would ask you to transfer the amount to our account no. … with Stadtsparkasse Wuppertal.
2.	Als Anlage erhalten Sie unseren Scheck über 463,– € als zweite Rate.	We are sending you enclosed our cheque for the amount of Euro 463.00 as the second instalment.
3.	Der Vergleich mit unseren Unterlagen hat eine Differenz von EUR 8,37 zu Ihren Gunsten ergeben.	When checking our records we noticed a difference of € 8.37 in your favour.
4.	Nachdem Sie uns nun seit über einem Jahr auf der Basis von Zahlung bei Rechnungserhalt beliefern, möchten wir Sie um offenes Zahlungsziel bitten.	As you have now been supplying us on the basis of payment on receipt of invoice for more than a year, we would like to ask you to grant us open credit.
5.	Wie vereinbart, haben wir einen 90-Tage-Wechsel auf Sie gezogen. Wir bitten Sie, diesen mit Ihrem Akzept zu versehen und an uns zurückzuschicken.	As agreed, we have dawn on you at 90 days' sight. Please return the draft provided with your acceptance.
6.	Die Royal Trade Bank wird Ihnen die Dokumente gegen Einlösung unserer Sichttratte aushändigen.	The Royal Trade Bank will surrender the documents against payment of our sight draft.
7.	Wir haben unsere Bank angewiesen, ein unwiderrufliches Akkreditiv zu Ihren Gunsten zu eröffnen, das bei einer Bank in Toronto zahlbar und bis 15. Oktober gültig ist.	We have instructed our bank to open an irrevocable letter of credit in your favour which is payable at a Bank in Toronto and valid until 15 October.
8.	Das Akkreditiv ist benutzbar gegen Vorlage folgender Dokumente in vierfacher Ausfertigung:	The letter of credit is available against presentation of the following documents in quadruplicate:

INFO: IBAN and BIC

IBAN:

Since 2001 the International Bank Account Number (IBAN) has been used in international payments in the European countries, improving the level of automation in cross-border payments and ensuring the proper arrival of payments.

The IBAN used in Germany has 22 characters and consists of

1. the country code for Germany DE
2. a 2-digit verifier
3. the 8-digit bank code
4. the 10-digit account number

Example:

DE88 5008 0400 0012 3456 78 (on a printed invoice)
DE88500804000012345678 (in electronic format)

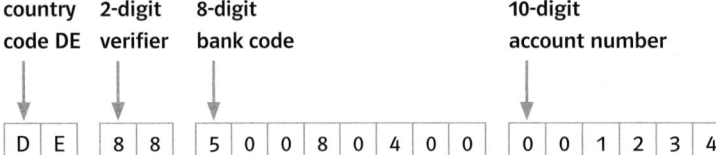

country code DE	2-digit verifier	8-digit bank code	10-digit account number

SWIFT BIC:

Payments by bank transfer are processed by the Society for Worldwide Interbank Financial Telecommunication (SWIFT), a co-operative founded by the banking industry in 1973. It supplies standardised messaging services and interface software to more than 10,000 financial institutions in 210 countries. The SWIFT BIC (Bank Identifier Code) identifies precisely the financial institutions involved in financial transactions. It has 8 characters and consists of

the 4-digit bank code

the 2-digit country code

the 2-digit location code

Example: BABADESA (Bayernbank + Deutschland + Ortskennzahl)

D | Avoiding common mistakes

Wrong	Correct
1. showing a balance of €17.20 ~~to~~ our favour	1. showing a balance of €17.20 **in** our favour
2. We have ~~transfered~~ the amount ~~on~~ your account ~~by~~ XYZ bank.	2. We have **transferred** the amount **to** your account **with** XYZ bank.
3. Checking your invoice we ~~noted~~ the following error.	3. Checking your invoice we **noticed** the following error.
4. Please ~~notice~~ that part shipments are not allowed.	4. Please **note** that part shipments are not allowed.
5. As we ~~are~~ now ~~doing~~ business ~~since~~ two years…	5. As we **have now been doing** business **for** two years…
6. We will ~~duely~~ honour the bill ~~by~~ maturity.	6. We will **duly** honour the bill **at** maturity.
7. Payment ~~should~~ be made by letter of credit.	7. Payment **is to** be made by letter of credit.
8. The bank will open a letter of credit, payable ~~by~~ a German bank and valid ~~up to~~ 31 July.	8. The bank will open a letter of credit, payable **at** a German bank and valid **until** 31 July.

Credit enquiries

A | Introduction

Some widely used terms of payment, such as 30 days net, open account, or documents against acceptance, actually grant the customer credit since the goods or services are supplied before payment
5 is effected. That is why suppliers need information about the customer's financial standing and payment record. Information on a company's creditworthiness can be obtained from the following sources:

10 – **Credit agencies** (US credit bureaus), which compile information from data which is publicly available such as companies' annual reports. The credit agency establishes a company profile and assesses the credit risk. Large companies have
15 online links to one or more credit agencies which provide them with real-time information on prospective customers.

Numerous big organisations exchange data on their customers' payment record on a regular basis.

20 – **The customer** himself, who fills in a questionnaire sent by the supplier.
– **Trade references**, i. e. other firms whom the customer has mentioned as a source of information.
– **Banks**, which, however, normally provide detailed
25 information to other banks only.
– **Chambers of commerce** and **consulates**.

Credit enquiries sent to trade references should be marked "private and confidential" and it should be emphasised that the company providing the
30 information will not be held responsible for this information and that it will be treated in strict confidence. At the end of the letter requesting information the writer will underline his willingness to reciprocate this service, should the
35 need arise.

Credit information

Giving information about a business partner is not without risks and companies may refuse to provide information. Especially when the information is not wholly positive, there is the
5 danger of a libel action. This is why even when giving favourable information you should – as a precaution –

– mark the letter as "private and confidential"
– stress that the information is given without
10 any obligation
– request confidential treatment
– use cautious expressions like "we believe", "in our opinion", "according to reliable sources", "it is said that ...", etc.

15 If the information you are giving is only lukewarm or is even unfavourable, the following additional precautions should be taken:

– refer to the name of the company about which you are giving information indirectly
20 ("the company in question") or type its name on a separate slip of paper
– avoid mentioning the precise amount of the credit line by referring to it as, say, "the figure mentioned in your letter".

B | Model letters

1 Structure of a detailed enquiry

Private and confidential ⬛ 1. note on confidentiality

Dear Ms Tomlinson ⬛ 2. appropriate salutation

Mr Peter Parker of Fashion World Ltd has given us your name as a trade reference. ⬛ 3. reference to the firm about which information is required

As we have had no previous dealings with this firm ⬛ 4. reason for enquiring

we would be most grateful if you could give ⬛ 5. information requested, e.g.
us information on their reputation, general ⬛ – reputation of its owners
management and payment record. ⬛ – business conduct
Above all we would like to know whether ⬛ – financial standing
you think it would be advisable to grant them ⬛ – creditworthiness
open credit terms for a period of 30 days ⬛ – volume of business done with them
on an order worth EUR 74,550. ⬛ – credit line suggested
⬛ – other relevant information

Any information you provide will, of course, be treated in strict confidence and without any obligation for you. ⬛ 6. promise to treat information confidentially and exclude any liability

We would be happy to be of assistance to you in a similar matter, should the occasion arise. ⬛ 7. offer to render a similar service

Yours sincerely ⬛ 8. complimentary close

2 Credit enquiry

Staffordshire Potteries plc Finest Bone China

Telford Road
Walton
ST7 11AD
Tel. +44 2078 30438
www.staffordshirepotteries.com

Max Maier
Bavaria Porzellan
Ludwigstr. 100
95100 Selb
Germany   06 May 201_

Private and confidential

Dear Mr Maier

We have been given your name by the German firm Stilfest GmbH in Esslingen as
a reference.

We have been doing business with that firm for just under a year on the basis of
cash on delivery. They have now approached us with the request for open account
terms with monthly settlement and suggested a credit line of € 4,500.

We would be very grateful for any information you may be able to provide regarding
their financial standing, conduct of business and payment habits. Any other
information you could furnish would also be very much appreciated.

Any information you provide will of course be treated in strict confidentiality and
without any liability on your side.

We shall be happy to render you a similar service any time if required.

Yours sincerely

Staffordshire Potteries plc

John Prendergast
Export Sales

3 Credit information

3.1 Favourable information

Bavaria Porzellan

Ludwigstr. 100 • 95100 Selb • Tel. +49 9287 804 71… • www.bavaria-porzellan… .de

Staffordshire Potteries plc
Telford Road
Walton
ST7 11AD
England   25 May 201_

Attn Mr John Prendergast
Export Sales
Private and confidential

Dear Mr Prendergast

In response to your letter of 22 May I am pleased to give you the following
information.

We have been trading with the company in question for over five years now and have
been granting them open account terms for the last four years. During this period
they have always settled their accounts on time and often taken advantage of cash
discount.
In our case, the sums involved are similar to the ones you mention in your letter.
We therefore think that we can safely say that you would not be taking any risks in
granting them the credit line you mentioned.

We have reason to believe that the company has a very sound financial standing.

We would like to point out that this opinion is based entirely on our own experience
and that we cannot assume any responsibility for the information given.

Yours sincerely
Bavaria Porzellan

Max Maier
Sales

3.2 Unfavourable information

Bavaria Porzellan

Ludwigstr. 100 • 95100 Selb • Tel. +49 9287 804 71… • www.bavaria-porzellan….de

Smykker og Bolig
Ellegardsvej 120
2820 Gentofte
Denmark   17 April 201_

For the attention of
Ms Merete Søderborg
Sales and Export

Private and confidential

Dear Ms Søderborg

Credit reference on your prospective customer

In reply to your enquiry of 12 April concerning a prospective customer in Germany
we should like to inform you that the last time we did business with this firm was
18 months ago. We therefore cannot give you any reliable information as to their
current financial standing.

Our past personal experience with the firm is not entirely positive as we had to send
them reminders to settle their account on several occasions.

We would therefore suggest that you proceed with caution when granting them
more favourable terms of payment.

However, we would like to emphasise that this information is based entirely on our
own past experience and may not reflect the firm's present financial position.

Please treat this information, which is given without any obligation whatsoever,
as strictly confidential.

Yours sincerely

Max Maier
Sales

C | Tool kit

1 Building blocks for business communications: Credit enquiries

To mention the source of address

We have	been given	your address	**by**	Messrs Wentworth & Sons
	received		**from**	as a reference.
	obtained			

Mrs Palmer has	given us your name as a trade reference.
	informed us that you are prepared to provide a reference.
	has recommended your credit agency **to** us.

As	this firm	is not known to us …
	this company	has never placed an order of that size …
	they are now asking for open account terms …

| Since we have not | done business with them so far … |
| | had any dealing with them before … |

To ask for information

We would be	pleased	if you could	give us	information	their	solvency.
	grateful		provide us **with**	**on** …	the company's	financial standing.
	obliged		supply		its	creditworthiness.
						business conduct.
						payment record.
						general performance.

Please	let us know	if they are solvent.
	tell us	how promptly they meet their financial obligations.
	indicate the volume of your business dealings with them.

Do you think it would be	advisable	to grant them	credit amounting to …
	reasonable		this credit line?
	in order		these credit facilities?

Any other	details	you may be able to supply will be appreciated.
	particulars	
	information	

To promise confidential treatment

You may be sure We assure you You have our word	that any information given will be	treated **as** strictly confidential handled with the utmost discretion	and	without any obligation for you. that you will not be held responsible for it. with no liability **on** your part.

To offer to reciprocate

If we can	do you a similar service be **of** assistance to you in a similar case return the favour	we shall be glad to reciprocate. please let us know. we will be pleased to do so.

2 Typical phrases (German/English): Credit enquiries

1. Sie wurden uns von Rushworth Industries als Referenz benannt.	Rushworth Industries have given us your name as a reference.
2. Zu Gegendiensten sind wir stets gern bereit.	We will be pleased to return the favour at any time.
3. Da wir mit dieser Firma bisher noch nicht in Geschäftsverbindung standen, möchten wir über sie Erkundigungen einziehen.	As we have not had any dealings with this firm before, we would like to obtain some information about them.
4. Wir wären Ihnen dankbar für Auskunft über die finanzielle Lage des Unternehmens sowie über sein Geschäftsgebaren und seine Zahlungsmoral.	We should be grateful for any information about the company's financial situation, their business conduct and their payment record.
5. Welchen Umfang hatten Ihre Geschäfte mit dieser Firma und wie pünktlich wurden Ihre Rechnungen beglichen?	What has been the volume of your dealings with this firm and how punctually have your invoices been settled?
6. Sind Sie der Meinung, dass wir dieser Gesellschaft eine Kreditlinie in dieser Höhe einräumen sollten?	Are you of the opinion that this firm can be safely granted a credit line for this amount?
7. Wir versichern Ihnen, dass alle Auskünfte streng vertraulich behandelt werden.	We assure you that any information will be treated strictly confidentially.
8. Mr. James Allen hat uns wegen einer Referenz an Sie verwiesen.	Mr James Allen has referred us to you regarding a reference.
9. Wir sind besonders daran interessiert zu erfahren, ob Rechnungen pünktlich bezahlt werden.	We are especially interested to learn whether invoices have been settled punctually.
10. Selbstverständlich werden diese Angaben für Sie vollkommen unverbindlich bleiben.	Any information given will, of course, be without any obligation to you.

3 Building blocks for business communications: Credit information

To refer to the company in question

The company	mentioned **on** the enclosed slip …	
	referred **to** in your letter …	
	in question …	

To give favourable information

We believe		is financially sound.
We are informed	that the company	is in a good financial state.
There is no doubt		has sufficient capital resources.

	proprietors	enjoy an excellent reputation.
The	owners	have a good track record.
	directors	are respectable and trustworthy business partners of ours.

To give non-committal information

We have only been doing business with this firm	**for** a few months	and are **for** this reason not in **a** position to say anything specific.
	on a very modest scale	
	on cash with order terms	

To give unfavourable information

It is said		is financially insecure.
We have heard		is experiencing financial difficulties.
It is generally known	that this company	is in a precarious financial position.
There are reports		may not have sufficient resources.
It seems		is finding it hard to meet its commitments.
Our impression is		is more or less insolvent.

According to reliable sources	the firm	is settling its accounts only with delays.
		has suffered heavy losses.
		does not seem to have a sound financial basis.
	one of their major customers has gone bankrupt.	

To make recommendations

We would, therefore,	recommend **that** you	perhaps demand that collateral is provided.
	advise you to	do business **on** cash terms only.
	suggest **that** you	proceed with caution **in** your dealings with this firm.
		obtain further information **from** their bankers or a credit agency.

To exclude liability and request confidential treatment

Please note that this	opinion	is given without any obligation on our part.
	information	
	recommendation	

We would remind you We expressly point out	that this information must be treated confidentially.

We trust that you will Please We would ask you to	treat this information	with the utmost discretion. as confidential. in strict confidence.

4 Typical phrases (German/English): Credit information

1.	Mit Bezug auf Ihr Schreiben vom 29. Dezember möchten wir Ihnen mitteilen, dass die genannte Firma seit fünf Jahren zu unseren Kunden zählt.	With reference to your letter of 29 December we would like to inform you that the company in question has been a customer of ours for five years.
2.	Wir bitten Sie, diese Angaben, für die wir keinerlei Verantwortung überneh-men, vertraulich zu behandeln.	Please treat this information, which is given without any obligation on our part, as confidential.
3.	Da wir erst seit wenigen Monaten mit dieser Firma in Geschäftsverbindung stehen, können wir leider keine fun-dierte Aussage machen.	As we have only been doing business with this company for a few months, we are not in a position to provide any well-founded information.
4.	Es heißt allgemein, dass sich das Unternehmen in einer äußert schwie-rigen Lage befindet, nachdem einer seiner wichtigsten Kunden Konkurs angemeldet hat.	It is generally said that the company is in a precarious financial position following the insolvency of one of their major customers.
5.	Wir würden Ihnen daher empfehlen, Sicherheiten zu verlangen, bevor Sie Kredit gewähren.	We would, therefore, recommend that you demand collateral before granting them credit.
6.	Wir sind der Meinung, dass das Unter-nehmen auf einer soliden finanziellen Basis steht.	We believe that the firm is financially sound.
7.	Die Firma ist ihren Zahlungsver-pflichtungen stets pünktlich nachge-kommen.	The company has always met its payment commitments punctually.
8.	Allem Anschein nach verfügt die Firma nicht über genügend Kapital.	It seems that the firm may not have sufficient capital.
9.	Die in Ihrer Anfrage genannte Firma genießt einen ausgezeichneten Ruf.	The company mentioned in your enquiry enjoys an excellent reputation.
10.	Seit einem halben Jahr gehen die Zahlungen nur schleppend ein.	There have been delays in payment for the last six months.

D | Avoiding common mistakes

Wrong	Correct
1. Ms Price has recommended ~~us~~ your credit agency.	1. Ms Price has recommended your credit agency **to us**.
2. Since we ~~are not doing~~ business with this firm so far …	2. Since we **have not done** business with this firm so far …
3. … please give us information on ~~it's~~ financial standing.	3. … please give us information on **its** financial standing.
4. Any ~~informations~~ given will be treated as confidential.	4. Any **information** given will be treated as confidential.
5. Please treat this information ~~strict confidential~~.	5. Please treat this information **strictly confidentially**.
6. The owners are trustworthy business partners of ~~us~~.	6. The owners are trustworthy business partners of **ours**.
7. We have been doing business with them ~~to~~ cash with order terms.	7. We have been doing business with them **on** cash with order terms.
8. One of their ~~mayor~~ customers has gone bankrupt.	8. One of their **major** customers has gone bankrupt.
9. We would suggest ~~to proceed~~ with caution.	9. We would suggest **that you proceed** with caution.

Delivery

A | Introduction

With the introduction of the Single Market, i. e. the free movement of goods, services, capital and people, the concept of import and export for trade within the EU was abolished and replaced by the
5 concept of intra-Community delivery of goods. A shipment of goods by a trader in one EU member state to a trader in another EU member state qualifies as an intra-Community delivery if

– both traders are registered for VAT in their
10 respective EU countries and
– the customer's and the supplier's VAT registration numbers are quoted on the invoice.

If this is the case the supplier may deliver the goods to the trader in the other member state without
15 charging VAT.

Domestic trade and trade within the EU Single Market are more straight-forward than trading on world markets. Some of the main reasons are:

20 – Regulations regarding product specifications are often different necessitating modifications to the product.
– There may be restrictions on the provision of services.
25 – Cultural differences may also require modifications to the product or packaging (localisation).
– There are more people involved in a given transaction.
30 – The risk of non-payment is greater so that it is important to choose a secure means of payment.
– There is a greater choice of trade terms.
– There is a currency risk – the Euro was designed to do away with exchange rate risk between
35 participating countries. Outside the Eurozone the risk remains.
– Transport over long distances (especially over land and sea) heightens the risk of loss or damage
– Language and cultural differences make
40 communication more difficult and misunderstandings more likely.
– There may be more government controls and regulations in the target country that must be observed.

B | Model letter: Dispatch advice (structure)

Bavaria Porzellan

Ludwigstr. 100 • 95100 Selb • Tel. +49 9287 804 71... • www.bavaria-porzellan... .de

Kinnock & Blythe
56 Donaghadee Bdwy
BELFAST BT21 8LL
Northern Ireland   23 April 201_

Dear Ms O'Connor   **1. appropriate salutation**

Your order 2-044-89778 dated 19 April 201_   **2. reference to order**

I am pleased to inform you that the items you ordered are now ready for dispatch.
We will be using Shamrock International for the delivery of your consignment which
will be collected from our warehouse on 26 April 201_. Delivery will take place
within 2 working days from the date of dispatch.
3. information that the goods are ready for collection or have been dispatched

The estimated delivery date will be 28 April 201_.   **4. estimated delivery date**

Please do not hesitate to contact me on the above number if there are any problems
or queries.   **5. offer to help in case of problems**

I would appreciate it if you could send me a brief note by email confirming that you
have received the consignment in good condition.   **6. request for confirmation**

I enclose a brochure on our updated programme for immediate delivery and look
forward to hearing from you soon.   **7. enclosure and goodwill phrase**

Yours sincerely   **8. complimentary close**

Carolina Misinsky
Carolina Misinsky
Exports
Enc

C | Tool kit

1 Building blocks for business communications: Delivery

To arrange for transport

| Please quote your | lowest best most favourable | rates tariffs | for | a single shipment regular shipments | **of** … |

| What is your tariff What do you charge | for transporting … | **by** | air rail lorry cargo liner ro-ro ferry | **to** … |

| We wish to charter We are interested in chartering | a | ship plane | of approx. 20,000 GRT. with a cargo capacity of 200 metric tons. |

To take out insurance

We would like to take **out** insurance for the transport of … to …

Please let us know **on** what terms you can provide cover for a consignment of …

The goods are to be insured against all risks, including war risk, SR & CC.

2 Building blocks for business communications: Dispatch advice

To say that the goods are ready for collection

| We are pleased | to inform you to advise you to let you know | that the consignment | is ready for collection. can be collected at our Derby works. |

To say that the goods have been dispatched

| The consignment has The merchandise has The machines have | now today this morning | been handed over to the freight forwarder. been sent **by** courier. left our premises **for** Budapest **by** lorry. |

| The goods have now been | dispatched shipped forwarded | **by** | air freight. inland waterway vessel. refrigerated truck. |

Yesterday the goods were loaded on board MS Seagull in Bremerhaven.

To give particulars about the transport

| The consignment | will arrive **at** your warehouse is expected to reach you is scheduled to be delivered | tomorrow afternoon. **on** Wednesday. **by** 17 January. |

MS Island Queen is	due to leave Antwerp **on** … and	dock **at** arrive in/at	Singapore **on** …

Estimated time of arrival: on or about 29 December.

Flight No. SA6941 will depart **from** Johannesburg International Airport **at** 20:35 (local time) **on** Monday and land **at** Frankfurt Airport **at** 6:10 on Tuesday.

To give particluars about packing

As requested According **to** your instructions As usual	the goods are packed in	strong solid sturdy	seaworthy containers. wooden crates. cardboard boxes with steel bands. metal drums. polythene bags.

To refer to payment

Our	statement for the first quarter invoice No. A/17, dated 2 March,	is enclosed **for** settlement

We enclose invoice No. A/17 **of** 2 March in duplicate and would ask you to transfer the amount in question to	the account given below. our account **with** CountyBank.

We have drawn **on** you for the invoice amount **at** 60 days and enclose the draft for your acceptance.

To refer to documents

The documents required under the letter of credit have been handed over to our bank.

We are sending you enclosed copies of the following documents: … . The originals will be released to you by your bank against payment.

To close a dispatch advice

We hope the consignment will arrive	punctually. safely and in good condition. in good time.

Thank you once again for this order. We should be very pleased if you would contact us again in the event of further requirements.

Please do not hesitate to contact us should you have any further requirements in the future.

3 Typical phrases (German/English): Delivery

1. Die 15 Kartons stehen ab Dienstag zur Abholung in unserem Lager in Ulm bereit.	The 15 cartons will be ready for collection from our warehouse in Ulm by Tuesday.
2. Die Maschine wurde gestern von der MS Poseidon in Hamburg an Bord genommen.	Yesterday the machine was loaded on board MS Poseidon in Hamburg.
3. Die bestellten Ersatzteile sind heute früh per Luftfracht an Sie abgegangen.	The spare parts ordered were dispatched to you by airfreight this morning.
4. Voraussichtliche Ankunftszeit: 20:45 Ortszeit, Flughafen Sao Paulo.	Estimated time of arrival: 20:45 local time, Sao Paulo airport.
5. Bitte teilen Sie uns mit zu welchen Bedingungen Sie die o.g. Sendung gegen alle Gefahr versichern können.	Please advise us on what terms you can insure the above-mentioned consignment against all risks.
6. Bitte geben Sie uns Ihre günstigsten Tarife für den Transport von 1500 Paar Schuhen auf dem Luftweg nach Tallinn in Estland an.	Please let us have your most favourable tariffs for the transport of 1,500 pairs of shoes by air to Tallinn in Estonia.

D | Avoiding common mistakes

Wrong	Correct
– Transport ~~with~~ lorry …	– Transport **by** lorry
– We ~~like~~ to charter a ship for the transport of…	– We **would like** to charter a ship for the transport of …
– We wish to ~~conclude~~ insurance for …	– We wish to **take out** insurance for …
– Please contact the ~~insurance~~.	– Please contact the **insurance company**.
– Please let us know ~~to~~ what terms you can insure a cargo of …	– Please let us know **on** what terms you can insure a cargo of …
– The goods will be sent ~~with~~ courier.	– The goods will be sent **by** courier.
– The truck left our premises ~~to~~ Paris last night.	– The truck left our premises **for** Paris last night.
– The consignment will arrive ~~by~~ your warehouse ~~at~~ 14 June.	– The consignment will arrive **at** your warehouse **on** 14 June.
– The documents will be released to you ~~from~~ your bank.	– The documents will be released to you **by** your bank.
– We hope the goods will arrive ~~punctual~~.	– We hope the goods will arrive **punctually**.

13 Complaints

Complaints and adjustments

A | Introduction

If there is something wrong with a consignment or transaction, the customer should inform the seller immediately. Often it will be enough to telephone or
5 send an e-mail for the supplier to suggest a solution to the problem. However, if the problem is more serious or the customer feels that his complaint is not being taken sufficiently seriously, he may decide to
10 write a letter of complaint.

The complaint should include the facts and give all the necessary details including the order and invoice number, the date of delivery and the nature of
15 the problem, such as damage to the consignment, delivery of the wrong goods, or delay in delivery etc. The complaint should also emphasise the inconvenience or loss that the customer
20 has suffered. It should suggest a method

of adjustment and request the seller to take immediate steps to compensate him. In some cases the customer will have to point out legal implications where 25 the contract provides for damages in the case of non-performance or delayed performance on the part of the supplier.

Finally, it is important to emphasise that a complaint should be unemotional and 30 polite but, at the same time, firm. However annoying the inconvenience caused, the complaint should not express anger. The customer should not lose sight of the fact that his aim is to get the seller to 35 rectify the problem.

B | Model e-mail: Apology and adjustment

To:
From:

Dear Mr H Meyer,

We are sorry to note you have not received your order. We attribute this incidence of non delivery/delay to ExpressMail. Your order should have arrived by now even if it was delayed.

We will therefore issue you a full refund within 48 hours as it is now past our estimated time of arrival and we do not wish to keep you waiting any longer.

Please be kind enough to contact us if/when this order is received.

We appreciate your business and apologise for any inconvenience this may have caused, as we know what it feels like not to receive an anticipated order.

You are a valued customer and we are committed to providing you with the best service possible.

Kind regards,
Anita Ravenscroft
The Oakwood Books Team

Oakwood Books – an environmentally-friendly company with the widest selection of books, CDs, DVDs, and a reputation for our friendly, courteous and prompt customer service.

C | Tool kit

1 Building blocks for business communications: Complaints

To start a complaint

I am writing We are writing	about with reference to regarding	our order no. …	, which	has reached us we received was delivered	today. yesterday. on …

We are sorry Much to our regret we have	to inform you that	the units have not yet reached us. we are still waiting for the consignment. the parcel has not yet arrived.

To point out positive aspects

The crate Container no. 3 The other parcels	contained	the correct equipment the goods ordered the items required	and	arrived reached us	in good condition.

To give reasons for your complaint

However,	one article unit no. …	is	badly seriously completely partly slightly	damaged. defective. bent. dented. scratched. broken. stained. cracked.
We are afraid We regret to inform you	that the following items	are		

When we unpacked the On examining the Inspecting the When we opened the	goods, cases, packages,	we	found discovered realised saw	that	two items were missing. they contained the wrong goods. the quality was below standard. one box was empty. there was a shortfall in weight of 7 kgs. you have delivered more units than we ordered.

We are afraid We must point out	that	the work performed is **below** standard. your services have been rather unsatisfactory. the repair work has been poorly executed.

To provide evidence

As evidence To illustrate our claim	we are enclosing we are sending as an attachment	samples of … the survey report **by** Messrs. … photographs of the faulty items. the carrier's receipt.

To mention likely reasons for the problem

We	believe think are sure	that the	delay damage breakage	is due to was caused **by** occured **through**	inadequate storage. rough handling in transit. faulty workmanship. an error in packing. careless execution of the order.
There is little doubt It is quite obvious				

Apparently, our order was mixed up with another customer's order.

To inform the seller what you expect them to do and what steps you are taking

Please ensure that we receive Please make sure that we are sent Please arrange for the dispatch of	the replacements the missing items suitable substitutes an updated version	immediately. without delay. as soon as possible.

We would ask you to	compensate us for the loss by granting us a discount of 20 %. release us from the contract.		
	replace	the faulty goods	by faultless ones at your expense.
	have		repaired as soon as possible. collected at our warehouse.

The wrongly delivered goods The defective machine The faulty components	will be kept	**in** our warehouse **at** your disposal	**until** further instructions from you. we hear from you.

The defective items will be returned to you at your risk and expense.

We are prepared to keep the	soiled damaged wrongly delivered	articles if you	grant us a price reduction **of** 5 %. indemnify us **for** the loss. cut the price **to** £560.00.

To demand prompt adjustment

Please look into this matter immediately and make suggestions **as to how** to settle it.

We	are convinced expect trust	that you will	be able to sort this out in the very near future. settle this matter speedily and **to** our entire satisfaction. adjust this business without further delay. send the replacements **by** the next available flight.

2 Typical phrases (German/English): Complaints

1. Wir nehmen Bezug auf unseren Auftrag Nr. AB4 vom 27.11.20_, den wir heute morgen erhalten haben.	We refer to our order No. AB4 of 27 November 201_ which we received this morning.
2. Kiste 3 enthielt 200 Teile, die wir nicht bestellt hatten.	Case no. 3 contained 200 components which we had not ordered.
3. Beim Auspacken von Paket 2 stellten wir leider fest, dass 10 Stück fehlten.	On unpacking parcel no. 2 we were disappointed to find that 10 items were missing.
4. Wir bedauern Ihnen mitteilen zu müssen, dass die Sendung noch nicht angekommen ist.	We regret to inform you that the consignment has not yet arrived.
5. Leider müssen wir Ihnen mitteilen, dass 24 Teile stark zerkratzt sind.	Unfortunately, we have to inform you that 24 units are badly scratched.
6. Wir müssen Sie darauf aufmerksam machen, dass wir mit der Ausführung der Reparatur nicht zufrieden sind.	We have to point out that we are dissatisfied with the execution of the repair work.
7. Zum Beweis fügen wir diesem Schreiben das Schadensgutachten bei.	As evidence we are enclosing the survey report.
8. Höchstwahrscheinlich ist der Schaden auf unsachgemäße Behandlung beim Transport zurückzuführen.	The damage is most likely due to rough handling during transport.
9. Wir bitten Sie die schadhaften Teile abholen zu lassen und uns unverzüglich Ersatz zu senden.	Please have the defective parts collected and send us replacements without delay.
10. Wir sind bereit die mangelhafte Ware zu behalten, sofern Sie uns einen Preisnachlass von 50 % gewähren.	We are prepared to keep the faulty goods provided you grant us a price reduction of 50 %.
11. Wir behalten die Teile hier, bis Sie uns weitere Anweisung erteilen.	We will keep the units here until we receive further instructions from you.
12. Bitte kümmern Sie sich sofort um diese Angelegenheit und lassen Sie uns wissen, wie Sie sie zu regeln gedenken.	Please look into this matter immediately and let us know how you intend to settle it.
13. Wir hoffen, dass Sie die Sache zu unserer Zufriedenheit und ohne jede weitere Verzögerung bereinigen werden.	We hope you will settle the matter to our satisfaction and without any further delay.
14. Anscheinend wurden zwei Bestellungen verwechselt und wir haben die für einen anderen Kunden bestimmten Bücher erhalten.	Apparently two orders were mixed up and we have received the books destined for another customer.
15. Insgesamt beträgt das Fehlgewicht 23,5 kg.	The shortage in weight amounts to 23.5 kg.

3 Building blocks for business communications: Replies to complaints

To refer to the complaint

We	acknowledge receipt of have received	your letter **of** … concerning your order No. 324. your e-mail and thank you for the information **about** …

Thank you for your e-mail drawing a serious problem to our attention.

We refer to your telephone call informing us **about** the breakdown of the conveyor belt.

To apologise

		the trouble you have had.
Please accept our apologies		what has happened.
We sincerely apologise	for	any inconvenience this may have caused.
We are very/extremely sorry		the poor service.
		the misunderstanding.

To explain the problem or promise to investigate it

We have now discovered We have looked into the matter and found	the mistake was made by our sub-contractors. the oversight happened in the dispatch department. the mix-up was the result of an error on our part.

The reason is that	we were short of staff during the holiday season. due to last-minute technical modifications shipment had to be delayed. a fire broke out in our warehouse. inadequate packing material was used.

As a result of	the holiday season a software problem an error **by** our supplier	your order could not be executed	as usual. **in** time. as stipulated.

We will investigate the matter thoroughly and inform you **of** our findings and the remedies taken.

To suggest a solution

We are pleased to say We are glad to inform you	that	your order a suitable substitute the consignment the products	will be dispatched on Monday. have/has been handed over to our freight forwarders. is/are now on its/their way to you.

The faulty articles will be exchanged for faultless ones.

To	retain your custom make **up for** the inconvenience caused compensate you for the loss	we are willing	to undertake the repairs free of charge. to grant you a price reduction of 20 %.

Although we are not	**at** fault to blame responsible for the delay	we are prepared to release you from the contract.

As an agreement seems difficult to reach, we would suggest referring the matter to arbitration.

To inform the buyer what you expect him to do

Please	keep the goods refrigerated until the arrival of our representative. return the faulty items carriage forward. send us all the evidence you have.

We will make this concession if you are prepared to keep the goods.

To promise that things will improve

We	promise assure you	that we will	make every effort to guarantee make sure do our utmost to ensure	that	your orders are given priority. this does not happen again. similar occurrences are rendered impossible.

To close on a note promoting good will

We hope that	the matter can be settled amicably. the solution suggested will find your approval. this proposal will help to satisfy all parties concerned.

We regret that we cannot meet your wishes in full and hope this will not impair our business relations.

We hope you will understand our situation and thank you for your patience **in** this matter

To reject a claim

We note with regret that you	feel obliged find it necessary	to complain **about** the	execution of the maintenance-work. quality of the equipment.

As Since	we	are **in** no way to blame are not **at** fault have fulfilled the contract down to the dot	we	have no alternative **but** to refuse have to reject are afraid we cannot accept	your claim.

We suggest that you	report take up	the matter	to with	the forwarders. the insurance company. our representative in …

After	careful thorough	examination investigation	of	the case your complaint the matter	we must	say point out inform you	that	the responsibility **for** this unfortunate affair does not lie **with** us. your order was carried out in accordance **with** the contract. we cannot be held liable **for** the damage.

4 Typical phrases (German/English): Adjustments

1.	Wir bestätigen den Eingang Ihres Schreibens vom 09.12.201_ und danken Ihnen dafür, dass Sie uns auf dieses Problem aufmerksam gemacht haben.	We have received your letter of 9 December 201_ and thank you for drawing this problem to our attention.
2.	Wir möchten uns für dieses Versehen vielmals entschuldigen.	We would like to offer our sincerest apologies for this oversight.
3.	Wir haben den Fall untersucht und festgestellt, dass die Schwierigkeiten auf ein Softwareproblem bei unserem Lieferanten zurückzuführen sind.	We have investigated the matter and found that the difficulties are due to a software problem of our supplier.
4.	Wir freuen uns Ihnen mitteilen zu können, dass die Ersatzlieferung noch heute an Sie abgeht.	We are pleased to inform you that the replace-ment delivery will be dispatched to you today.
5.	Da wir Sie für die Ihnen entstandenen Unannehmlichkeiten entschädigen möchten, sind wir bereit, Ihnen einen Preisnachlass von 15 % zu gewähren.	As we would like to compensate you for the inconvenience caused we are prepared to grant you a discount of 15%.
6.	Wenn Sie sich entschließen die Teile zu behalten, werden wir den Preis auf $27,50 pro Stück ermäßigen.	Should you decide to keep the components we will reduce the price to USD 27.50 per unit.
7.	Wir versichern Ihnen, dass wir alles daran setzen werden, unseren Service zu verbessern.	We assure you that we will do our utmost to improve our service.
8.	Bitte haben Sie Verständnis dafür, dass wir Ihre Beschwerde zurückweisen müssen, da uns keinerlei Schuld an diesem Transportschaden trifft.	Please understand that we have to reject your complaint as we are by no means to blame for the transport damage.
9.	Wir hoffen, dass diese Angelegenheit damit zu Ihrer Zufriedenheit erledigt worden ist und würden gerne wieder für Sie tätig werden.	We hope that the matter has been settled to your satisfaction and would like to serve you again.
10.	Alle fehlerhaften Artikel werden sofort gegen einwandfreie ausgetauscht.	All the faulty articles will be immediately exchanged for perfect ones.

D | Avoiding common mistakes

Wrong	Correct
– I refer to our order ~~about~~ steel tubes.	– I refer to our order **for** steel tubes.
– The parcel ~~arrived not yet~~.	– The parcel **has not yet arrived**.
– One article is ~~complete~~ damaged.	– One article is **completely** damaged.
– As an attachment we are sending you the report ~~of/from~~ the inspection agency.	– As an attachment we are sending you the report **by** the inspection agency.
– The ~~damages are~~ due to rough handling.	– The **damage** is due to rough handling.
– Please arrange for the ~~immediately~~ dispatch.	– Please arrange for the **immediate** dispatch.
– Please replace the faulty goods ~~with~~ faultless ones ~~to~~ your expense.	– Please replace the faulty goods **by** faultless ones **at** your expense.
– We will keep the goods ~~to~~ your disposal.	– We will keep the goods **at** your disposal.
– The goods will be returned ~~to~~ your risk and expense.	– The goods will be returned **at** your risk and expense.
– Please make suggestions ~~how~~ to settle the matter.	– Please make suggestions **as to how** to settle the matter.
– We wish to ~~excuse us~~ for this oversight.	– We wish to **apologize** for this oversight.
– The problem lies ~~by~~ shipping department.	– The problem lies **with** the shipping department.
– The faulty articles will be exchanged ~~with/through~~ faultless ones.	– The faulty articles will be exchanged **for** faultless ones.
– We would suggest ~~to refer~~ the matter to arbitration.	– We would suggest **referring/that we refer** the matter to arbitration.
– We will make this concession if you ~~will be~~ prepared to keep the goods.	– We will make this concession if you **are** prepared to keep the goods.
– We hope this will satisfy all ~~concerned parties~~.	– We hope this will satisfy all **parties concerned**.
– We have no alternative ~~than~~ to refuse your claim.	– We have no alternative **but** to refuse your claim.
– The responsibility ~~of~~ this unfortunate affair does not lie ~~by~~ us.	– The responsibility **for** this unfortunate affair does not lie **with** us.

 Useful tips: Complaints and adjustments

Making complaints

If your complaint is to be successful, you should

– inform the seller without delay
– whenever possible personalise the salutation
– provide all the necessary information, such as order number and date, etc.
– describe the problem in detail as objectively as possible
– supply evidence, if possible, by providing photographs, documents etc.
– stress the inconvenience caused
– suggest a solution asking either for a discount, replacements or substitutes etc.
– ask for immediate action.

Remember your complaint is more likely to achieve results if the tone of your correspondence is calm and polite, yet firm.

Reminders

A | Introduction

It is a relatively frequent occurrence that invoices are not settled on time. The seller must then take steps to persuade the buyer to pay the bill. He will be in a bit of a quandary – on
5 the one hand he wants to obtain payment but on the other he does not want to alienate his customer.

Thus, a reminder needs to be both persuasive and tactful. Often a telephone call (to take the
10 bull by the horns!) will be more effective than a letter or email. It gives the seller a chance to assess the customer's attitude of mind and gives the customer the opportunity to explain informally any difficulties he might be having.

15 However, often it is necessary to send several written reminders to achieve the desired result. They will gradually become more insistent in tone, the seller being mindful of the customer's payment record in the past. The interval
20 between the reminders may vary. They should contain a reference to the date and number of the invoice, the amount owed, how long the invoice is overdue and a request for payment within a given timeframe.

25 The first written reminder will often include a copy of the invoice or statement of account. Non-payment is not always the customer's fault so the first reminder should be positive, understanding and avoid blaming the customer.
30 This reminder may often be included in other correspondence (hidden reminder). If this fails to get results the second reminder will be more insistent. It should still be friendly, asking for an explanation but perhaps offering
35 help while requesting payment. If the supplier suggests he might reconsider terms of payment if the invoice remains unpaid, he should still emphasise that he wishes to continue business relations. The final reminder will appeal to the
40 customer's sense of fairness and also his desire to maintain his reputation by stressing the

consequences of non-payment. It will point out that the customer will also have to pay interest on arrears. The seller sets a final deadline for
45 payment and warns the customer that should he fail to meet the deadline he will either hand over the matter to a collection agency or instruct their solicitors. Here, too, it will generally be appropriate to express regret at
50 having to take this step.

In Germany four out of five claims for payment are settled through the simplified "gerichtlicher Mahnbescheid". There is no such specific order
55 for payment procedure in England and Wales. The creditor can, however, obtain a judgment by default (Versäumnisurteil) against the debtor as part of the normal civil court procedure ordering him to pay what is owed.

B | Model letters and model telephone conversation

1 Structure of a detailed reminder

Dear Mr Pratt   `1. personal salutation`

We refer to our e-mail of 30 October asking for settlement of our statement of account No. UK/140-77 of 30 September, which is now five weeks overdue.
`2. reference to invoice/statement of account/due date/`
`previous reminder(s), if applicable`

Apparently, the account has escaped your attention.
`3. suggestion of oversight on the debtor's part, if applicable`

As you have always paid your bills promptly, we are at a loss to understand this delay in payment.   `4. request for explanation, if appropriate`

Nevertheless we must ask you to remit the invoice amount within the next 10 days.   `5. request for payment, setting a deadline`

Should you fail to settle your account within this period, we will unfortunately have to reconsider the terms of payment.
`6. steps to be taken, unless payment is made`

We trust, however, that you will remit the outstanding amount in the next few days and that our cordial business relations can be continued.
`7. goodwill ending`

Yours sincerely   `8. complimentary close`

Enc. September Statement of Account   `9. enclosure, if applicable`

2 Structure of a detailed reply to a reminder

Dear Ms Osborne   1. personal salutation

We have received your fax of 20 November concerning your statement of account
No. UK/140-77   2. reference to reminder(s)

and would like to offer our sincere apologies for the delay in payment.   3. apologies

Unfortunately, three of our major customers have become insolvent in the last
few months due to the general decline in the domestic tourism industry. This has
obviously placed us in a somewhat precarious position.
4. explanation for the delay in payment

This is why we have to ask you for a respite of three weeks. Alternatively we could
pay half of the sum now and the rest in four weeks' time.
5. solution suggested:
– extension of due date
– down payment and payment of balance
at a later date
– payment by instalments

We hope you will understand our temporary predicament and see your way clear
to granting us this concession, particularly in view of our long-standing business
relations.   6. request for understanding

You may be sure that we will be in a position to settle the account in the way
suggested above as we are expecting major payments by our overseas customers
in the next few weeks.   7. assurance that payment will be made

We are very sorry for the inconvenience caused and look forward to receiving
your comments.   8. appropriate ending

Yours sincerely   9. complimentary close

3 Telephone conversation

AE: Good morning. Croydon Engineering Ltd, Alison Elliot speaking. How can I
help you?

SL: Good morning. This is Sven Lensing from Maschinenbau-Jost in Münster.
Could you put me through to Andrew Hamilton in Accounts, please.

AE: Certainly, Mr Lensing. I'll put you through to his extension. Oh, I'm afraid
his extension is busy. Would you like to hold?

SL: Yes, I would, but I am speaking from Germany.

AE: Of course, I'll keep trying. (After a short delay) I'm putting you through now.

AH: Good morning, Andrew Hamilton speaking.

SL: Hello Andrew, this is Sven from Maschinenbau-Jost. I'm ringing about our
invoice 14-XJ2032 for which payment was due exactly 2 months ago. We sent
you a reminder 5 weeks ago but I'm afraid we haven't heard anything

from you. So I thought I'd give you a ring to find out what the problem is instead of sending you another reminder. It's not like you to miss payment deadlines – and we have been doing business for at least ten years.

AH: Just a second I'll bring it up on my monitor. This is it – the invoice for €5,876.27 from 17 September. Yes, we haven't paid it yet. I'm afraid we are juggling a bit with payments at the moment as one of our biggest customers has gone bankrupt and a major customer in Argentina has defaulted on payment. So we are having cash flow problems. I'm really sorry about this. It's really very embarrassing.

SL: But why didn't you get in touch with me? You're a good customer and we've always had excellent business relations. We could have worked something out.

AH: I know, I ought to have rung you. I was hoping to be able to pay by the end of next week. We're also negotiating a bank loan to tide us over but it's not been finalised yet.

SL: OK, but we need to know when you're going to pay. We have our commitments as well.

AH: Of course. I could offer to pay half the sum outstanding within two weeks and the rest within a further two weeks.

SL: Alright – I've made a note of that. But be sure to contact me in good time if there are any problems.

AH: I'm sure that'll be OK. Thank you for being so understanding. I really am sorry that this situation has arisen but I'm afraid it is largely beyond our control. I hope we'll be able to place new orders in the near future.

SL: OK. Keep in touch. Look forward to hearing from you.

C | Tool kit

1 Building blocks for business communications: Reminders

To refer to the invoice/statement of account/previous reminder(s)

We refer to			statement of account for April.
We would like to	remind you **of**	our	invoice no. AB700 of 20 September.
	draw your attention **to**		letter dated 14 June.
			reminders of 14 and 30 June.

The invoice	was due **on** 31 July.
The sum of €20,359.00	is still outstanding.
The balance of $720.75	is now four weeks overdue.

The account shows a balance of €7,390 in our favour.

To suggest an oversight, request an explanation and/or express disappointment

As you have	never exceeded the credit period	we think		there must have been some misunderstanding.
	always paid punctually	we assume	that	you must have overlooked our invoice.
	always been a reliable business partner	we believe		you may have been prevented from paying by exceptional circumstances.

You have neither remitted the amount due nor given us any explanation for the delay in payment.

Given your previous excellent payment record we are wondering why you are withholding payment.

To demand payment and set a deadline

Please We would ask you to We must insist that you	clear the balance remit the amount settle the account make payment transfer the sum **of** € 4,220.00 send us a cheque **for** $ 375.50	without further delay. immediately. **by** the end of next week. **by** 7 May **at the latest**. **within** seven days. as agreed.

To point out the consequences of non-payment

Should you fail to If you do not Unless you	meet this deadline make payment **by** this date remit the amount **in** time	we	regret that we will have to are afraid we shall be forced to shall have no option but to

change our terms of payment.
supply you **on** "cash with order" terms in future.
terminate our business relations.
take legal steps.
institute legal proceedings.

hand the matter over to	our legal department. our solicitors. a collection agency.

To close a reminder

In the event that payment has already been effected in the meantime, please disregard this letter.

We would be grateful for We are looking forward to	an early settlement.

Please	let us know what arrangements you are making for payment. contact us immediately so that we can avoid an unpleasant situation.

We would be very sorry to lose a long-standing customer. So please make sure that the matter is settled to our mutual satisfaction.

2 Typical phrases (German/English): Reminders

1. Mit Bezug auf unsere Rechnung Nr. XZ34 vom 29. Dezember 201_ müssen wir Sie leider darauf aufmerksam machen, dass der Rechnungsbetrag von $620,– noch immer nicht bei uns eingegangen ist.	Referring to our invoice no. XZ34 of 29 December 201_ we must, unfortunately, point out that the invoice amount of $620.00 is still outstanding.
2. Wir bedauern Ihnen mitteilen zu müssen, dass Ihr Konto inzwischen einen Saldo von €16.820,55 zu unseren Gunsten aufweist und bitten Sie, das Konto unverzüglich auszugleichen.	Much to our regret we have to inform you that by now there is a balance of €16,820.55 in our favour on your account and would ask you to settle the account without further delay.
3. Da die Zahlung nun seit acht Wochen überfällig ist, sehen wir uns gezwungen, ein Inkassobüro mit der Angelegenheit zu betrauen.	As payment has now been overdue for eight weeks, we are obliged to hand the matter over to a collection agency.
4. Sofern Sie die Rechnung nicht bis spätestens 31. Juli begleichen, werden wir gerichtliche Schritte in Erwägung ziehen müssen.	Unless you effect payment by 31 July at the latest, we will have to consider taking legal action.
5. Es ist uns unverständlich, warum Sie uns keine Erklärung für das Ausbleiben der Zahlung gegeben haben.	We are at a loss to understand why you have not given us any explanation for the delay in payment.
6. Wir hoffen, die Angelegenheit kann zu unser aller Zufriedenheit erledigt werden.	We hope the matter can be settled to our mutual satisfaction.
7. Da Sie normalerweise pünktlich zahlen, gehen wir von einem Versehen aus.	As you have generally paid punctually, we assume that the invoice must have been overlooked.

3 Building blocks for business communications: Replies to reminders

To inform the supplier about payment

We will	transfer remit	€ ...			**to** your account.	
We have	transferred remitted	the amount the sum	due in question	**by**	SWIFT bank	transfer.
Enclosed you will find We are enclosing We are sending you	our cheque no. 3486 our banker's draft	**for** €	**in**	payment settlement	**of**	your invoice no. ... your statement of ...
	your bill of exchange at 60d/s, duly accepted.					

To refer to reminder(s)

We have received We acknowledge receipt of	your	invoice statement letter	of 2 May and thank you for	drawing the account to our attention. your patience.

To apologise

We sincerely apologise We are very sorry We offer our sincere apologies	**for** this	oversight. delay in payment. software failure.
	for the inconvenience caused by this state of affairs.	

We very much regret We are deeply sorry	that	there has been a delay in settling the account. you should have had to remind us of the due date. the invoice has become past due.

To mention the reasons for the delay in payment

Your invoice has not yet been paid	as a result of as a consequence of	a breakdown of our computer system. an error **by** our bank. an unexpected fall in demand. the sharp down turn in our industry. the unforeseen decline **in** e-commerce.

Payment has not been made	because	you charged us the wrong price.
		a major customer of ours: has gone bankrupt. / failed to meet his obligations. / has gone into compulsory liquidation.
		you sent us the wrong goods.

To ask for an extension and/or suggest an alternative

To our regret we are obliged to ask you		to grant us a respite of two months. for an extension of three weeks.
	to extend	the deadline **by** 10 days. the date of maturity of the draft **by** one month. the credit **on** your March statement.

We would suggest **that**	we remit €10,000 now and the balance in three months. we pay in three identical instalments of $30,330. we send you a cheque **for** £5,000 now and that you draw **on** us **at** 60 days for the rest.

To give assurances that payment will be effected

We assure you You may rest assured	that	payment will be effected promptly there will be no further delay in payment your invoice will then be paid in full	as	we are expecting a considerable payment from one of our debtors. there are clear signs that our situation is likely to improve shortly. business is already picking up noticeably.

To ask for understanding

In view of our long-standing business relations we would be grateful if you could We trust that you will understand our difficult situation and	make this concession. grant the respite requested. agree **to** our suggestions. find our proposal acceptable.

To close the letter

We hope that	future contacts will not be affected by this unfortunate affair our business relations will not be impaired by this	and look forward to your	comments. reply.

To grant the request for extension

Considering In view of Because of	our long-standing business relations the exceptional circumstances the guarantees you offered to provide	we are prepared to	agree to payment **by** instalments. grant the extension of credit. accept the solution suggested.

To offer a compromise and mention conditions

We have decided We are prepared	to accept a down payment of €1,500 to agree to your proposal	if you	remit the balance no later than 31 August. pay the remainder **by** 10 May. accept a draft **at** 30 days' sight.

To refuse the request for extension

We understand We are aware of	your difficulties but	are unfortunately not in **a** position to accommodate you are unable to extend the credit any further must to our regret insist **on** immediate payment

as since	the account is already six months overdue. we are obliged to meet our own commitments. this is the third time you have failed to balance your account within the agreed period.

4 Typical phrases (German/English): Replies to reminders

1. Hiermit teilen wir Ihnen mit, dass wir unsere Bank angewiesen haben, den Restbetrag von €430,75 auf Ihr Konto bei der Hampshire Bank zu überweisen.	Herewith we would like to inform you that we have instructed our bank to transfer the balance of €430.75 to your account with Hampshire Bank.
2. Zu meinem Bedauern muss ich Ihnen mitteilen, dass es mir momentan nicht möglich ist, Ihre Rechnung vom 30. Dezember in voller Höhe zu begleichen.	I regret having to inform you that I am currently unable to pay your invoice of 30 December in full.
3. Wir bedauern die Verzögerung und bitten um Entschuldigung für die Ihnen hierdurch entstandenen Unannehmlichkeiten.	We are very sorry for the delay and offer our sincere apologies for the inconvenience you have been caused.
4. Die Zahlung konnte noch nicht vorgenommen werden, da unsere eigenen Kunden wegen der Rezession im Einzelhandel unsere Rechnungen nur sehr schleppend begleichen.	Payment could not be effected because our own customers are very slow in paying our invoices as a result of the recession in the retail trade.
5. Ich hoffe, dass Sie sich angesichts unserer langjährigen Geschäftsbeziehungen in der Lage sehen, unserem Vorschlag zuzustimmen.	I hope that in view of our long-standing business relations you will agree to our suggestions.
6. Wir wären Ihnen sehr verbunden, wenn Sie damit einverstanden wären, dass eine Teilzahlung von £6,500 sofort erfolgt und der Rest im Laufe des Monats beglichen wird.	We would be grateful if you could agree to our proposal that we make a down payment of £6,500 immediately and remit the balance in the course of this month.
7. Da wir in Kürze den Eingang größerer Zahlungen erwarten, können Sie sich darauf verlassen, dass die Überweisung pünktlich erfolgt.	As we are expecting considerable sums in the near future, you may rest assured that the amount in question will be remitted punctually.
8. In Anbetracht unserer bisher so erfreulichen Geschäftsbeziehungen sind wir bereit, Ihnen diesmal entgegenzukommen.	Considering our excellent business relations so far we are prepared to accommodate you in this particular instance.
9. Wir können Ihre Schwierigkeiten durchaus nachvollziehen, dennoch ist es uns unmöglich, noch länger auf die Begleichung unserer Rechnung zu warten.	Although we are certainly aware of your difficulties, we are not in a position to wait any longer for the settlement of our invoice.

D | Avoiding common mistakes

Wrong	Correct
1. We refer to our invoice ~~about/over~~ €715.20 ~~from~~ 23 March.	1. We refer to our invoice **amounting to/in the amount of** €715.20 **of/dated** 23 March.
2. Our invoice ~~about~~ a consignment of books is still outstanding.	2. Our invoice **for** a consignment of books is still outstanding.
3. Please transfer ~~£25.750,50~~ to our account.	3. Please transfer **£25,750.50** to our account.
4. The invoice was due ~~at~~ 31 July.	4. The invoice was due **on** 31 July.
5. The account shows a balance of €65 ~~to~~ our favour.	5. The account shows a balance of €65 **in** our favour.
6. We suppose that you must have ~~overseen~~ our statement of account.	6. We suppose that you must have **overlooked** our statement of account.
7. Please settle the account ~~until~~ the end of the week.	7. Please settle the account **by** the end of the week.
8. The ~~due amount~~ has already been remitted.	8. The **amount due** has already been remitted.
9. ~~In the last time~~ we have also had problems collecting our outstanding accounts.	9. **Recently** we have also had problems collecting our outstanding accounts.
10. We suggest ~~to pay~~ in three ~~rates~~ of £2000 each.	10. We suggest **that we pay** in three **instalments** of £2000 each.
11. We are sure our situation will improve in ~~the next time~~.	11. We are sure our situation will improve **in the near future**.
12. We are, unfortunately, not in ~~the~~ position to grant you the respite.	12. We are, unfortunately, not in **a** position to grant you the respite.
13. We trust you will agree ~~with~~ our suggestions.	13. We trust you will agree **to** our suggestions.

Marketing and sales

A | Introduction

The pressure to deliver the right product at the right place at the right time has never been greater. The word "product" also includes services – banks, investment funds, insurance companies, etc. also speak of their products. **Marketing** is the tool designed to achieve the above objectives. It includes all the activities necessary to ensure a profitable demand for a product or service. Even when a product or service is still at the idea or design stage, companies set about finding out what sort of a market exists – for instance, what age group they should aim at and how likely people in this age group are to buy this product or service and what design or brand preferences they may have. Failure to assess the market correctly may lead to expensive mistakes.

Once a company has decided to launch a product, its success on the market will largely depend on the appropriate **marketing mix**, or four Ps (product, price, place, promotion), i.e. deciding on the product, deciding what price to charge and distribution channels to use – cheap chain or exclusive boutique, for instance. The positioning of the product in the right segment of the market, the batch sizes the firm is prepared to sell (how exclusive the product is), the quality of customer service all contribute to a product's success or failure. The company also has to decide where to advertise the product. The company's overall brand or image also plays an important role (exclusive luxury brand or mass-market product). Companies with an upmarket brand have to be careful not to destroy the brand's prestige by selling too cheaply through the wrong kind of outlet. A fashion retailer might alienate its young customers by projecting a traditional image and its older customers by appearing too trendy.

Public relations activities are designed to strengthen a company's image. The activities may include providing press releases for the media, sponsoring sports or cultural events, inviting the public to visit their premises on open days, making donations to charities and prestigious universities, funding ecological projects and getting involved in community affairs. These activities may be designed to define and enhance the firm's overall image. Often, however, they may be an element in the marketing mix for promoting a specific product. In the words of a PR analyst, "Advertising has become increasingly unaffordable for smaller companies, NGOs (**N**on-**G**overnmental **O**rganisations) and cultural institutions, for instance, with the result that media relations have begun to play an ever more important part in their marketing spend. Close personal relations with the press coupled with the professionalisation of press releases have proved to be excellent vehicles for reaching specific target groups."

B | Model letters/e-mail

1 Enquiry about co-operation

From: exports@deskgems... .de
To: ue.lipton@queensland-cc... .au
Date: 25 March 201_
Re: co-operation with Australian partners

Dear Ms Lipton,

I am contacting you because I think that the Queensland Chamber of Commerce might be able to help us find a suitable partner for co-operation, preferably under an agency agreement.

We are a German supplier of high-quality office accessories. Our product range is selling very well in most EU countries, Russia and the Gulf States. We now wish to boost our exports to Australia and New Zealand by establishing a representation for these countries. The company in question would have to sell our products on a commission basis, preferably through an existing network of retail outlets. I attach a file giving details of our range of products.

I would be grateful if you could recommend a suitable company or publish our offer in your monthly online bulletin.

Thank you very much for your help.

Best regards

DeskGems GmbH
Joachim Rautenstrauch
Head of Exports

Attachment: sales.lit.pdf

2 Informal marketing letter

In the fields of marketing and advertising, written communication is often rather informal. On the next page is an example of a letter sent to a potential customer by a business start-up:

Garden of Eden Rare and Subtropical Plants from Jersey

Janice Humble
Sales Manager
j.humble@gardenofeden.co... .uk
13 La Rue D'Aval
St Martin JE3 6UL
Jersey
JH/gl   12 August 201_

Sebastian Kluse
Der Grüne Daumen
Vegesacker Str. 88b
28773 Bremen
Germany

Dear Mr Kluse

Brighten up the winter gloom

As one of the leading garden centres in north-west Germany, you will be familiar
with what the situation will be like in a few months' time: the grey gloom of winter
will have us firmly in its grip, and your customers will just be desperate to escape
the January blues.

Well, we thought, let's do something about it! Sarah, Jessica, Bob and me decided
to put a little colour and magic into the foggy, rainy, chilly season and brighten up
our (plant) life.

Garden of Eden – that's us – is a nursery with a difference: for every climatic
condition and soil type, for indoors or outdoors, for dry, sunny, wet or shady spots –
we have just the right solution to brighten up even the darkest walled garden. Even
in mid-winter!
Take a look at our catalogue and be amazed by the colourful variety of quality
plants we offer and supply throughout the EU – from wonderfully fragrant winter
jasmine and stunning new cyclamen varieties to our exciting range of glossy-leaved
bamboos.
Visit our website and learn more about us. We offer a wide range of services with
expert advice on planting, growing, feeding and looking after your plants' health.
Sign up to our newsletter and stay in touch with what's going on and what's new
at **Garden of Eden**. Create your own account and make use of our attractive special
offers.

If you feel you need more information, just drop me a line and I'll get back to you
as quickly as possible.

I look forward to hearing from you soon.

Janice Humble (Sales Manager)

Enc. catalogue/price list

3 Offer to act as an agent

Office Empire
Thames Valley Ind. Est. – Bracknell – RG12 9TK – United Kingdom
+44 1344 889 350 2… – contact@officeempire.co… .uk

DeskGems GmbH
Rheinallee 201
68156 Mannheim
Germany

10 September 201_

Offer to act as an agent

Dear Mr Rautenstrauch,

We started importing your range of office accessories nine months ago and they have turned out to be a tremendous success in the UK. Our customers praise the stylish design, excellent craftsmanship and outstanding quality of your products and we receive regular requests for more product information.

As you will be aware, we have a large network of business partners and affiliates in this country, which gives us an excellent insight into the market for office accessories. We believe that there is a huge potential for your products and we would therefore be delighted to offer you our expertise and act as your agents for your entire product line.

We would like to suggest the following terms:

Start of our agency agreement: 6 October 201_ for an initial period of one year
Terms: open account with monthly statements payable 30 days after receipt
Storage: at our risk and expense
Commission: 20% to cover our expenses based on the invoice value CIF London-Gatwick

We would also appreciate it if you could give us your support for initial marketing activities.

For references regarding our credit standing please contact:
Ms Ruby Nasheer, Westminster Bank International, 44 Picadilly, London W1H 8TL

We look forward to hearing from you soon.

Yours sincerely

Oliver Parris
Oliver Parris
Head of Imports

C | Tool kit

1 Building blocks for business communications: Agencies

To apply for an agency

I have learned **from**	the Anglo-German Chamber of Commerce Mrs Harville of Harville & Partners your advertisement in The Industrialist			
that you are looking for	an agent for your products		in	Scotland the North of Bavaria Romania and Bulgaria
	someone	to represent your interests to market your services		
and I would like to	inform you that I would be prepared to assume the sole agency. offer my services. say that I am interested in distributing your products as your agent.			

To offer an agency

We are interested in	setting up an agency in your part of the country. finding a dynamic person to handle our sales in the Channel Islands. appointing a sole agent for our products.

To introduce yourself, your firm, your products or your services

I	have excellent connections in our industry. have been working successfully in this line for 15 years. have always achieved excellent sales figures.

Our company has	spacious premises including a large showroom. an extensive network of sales outlets all over the country. a highly motivated sales force.

We are	well-known Germany's leading one of the major	suppliers of accessories **for** the car industry. manufacturers of kitchen utensils. providers of e-commerce services.

Our	sound systems will satisfy your most discerning customers. products are unsurpassed both in quality and price. financial services are sure to find a ready market **among** professionals **on** high incomes.

To appoint an agent

We are pleased to We herewith	appoint you sole agent entrust you **with** the sole agency	for the whole of Italy.

To report to the principal

We are enclosing our	report for the 2nd quarter.
	account sales for January.
	sales figures for articles NZ12 and 14.

May I point out that	the figures have never been better in the last 5 years.
	sales have increased almost 200 %.
	this increase is the result of our good after-sales service.

The decline in sales is due to	fierce competition **from** Malaysia and Taiwan.	
	the fact that	your prices are 20 % above those of our competitors.
		we had to recall 1000 scooters because they were not safe.

The economic situation here	has unfortunately been deteriorating **over** the last few months.
	is now improving slowly.
	is still somewhat unsettled.

To ask the principal for support

I am afraid	sales will remain sluggish unless you cut your prices **by** at least 5 %.
	I must ask you for another €20,000 to finance the advertising campaign.
	this extremely valuable customer will have to be granted 25 % discount.

In view of my	outstanding results	
	excellent sales record	I think it would be only fair to raise my
	lead over the competitors	commission **to** 12 %.

To inform or instruct the agent

The new	prices will apply **as from** July 1st.
	improved version will not be introduced **before** March.
	advertising budget will have to be spread **over** 13 months.

Please bear in mind that	you must not handle systems of a competitive type.
	we require an accurate database of our customers at all times.
	your service engineers must be available day and night.

To modify or cancel the agency agreement

We are prepared to	increase your commission **by** 2.5 %.
	extend your territory to include the state of Saxony as well.
	prolong the agreement **for** another two years..

We think it best	to terminate the agreement **as of** 1st September
	to grant you a del credere commission of 2 %.
	to increase your advertising allowance **to** Euro 150,000 per year.

We hereby give due notice of the termination of the agency agreement with effect **from** 1st January 201_.

2 Typical phrases (German/English): Marketing and sales

1. Wir suchen eine zuverlässige Firma, die in der Lage ist, unsere Produkte auf dem deutschen Markt zu vertreiben.	We are looking for a reliable company that is in a position to distribute our products on the German market.
2. Wir wären an der Übernahme der Vertretung interessiert, da wir über ein dichtes Vertriebsnetz und gut ausgebildete Mitarbeiter verfügen.	We would be interested in representing your company as we have an extensive distribution network and a well-trained sales force.
3. Wir ernennen Sie hiermit zu unserem Alleinvertreter für das Gebiet der Republik Irland.	We herewith appoint you sales agent for the territory of the Republic of Ireland.
4. Bitte senden Sie uns unverzüglich Ihre Verkaufsabrechnung für das vierte Quartal.	Please send us your account sales for the fourth quarter without delay.
5. Der Rückgang der Absatzzahlen ist auf die unsichere politische Lage in unserem Land und die damit verbundene Rezession zurückzuführen.	The decline in sales is due to the instable political situation in our country and the resulting recession.
6. Die für das Frühjahr geplante Werbekampagne kann nur durchgeführt werden, wenn Sie unser Werbebudget für das kommende Jahr um ein Drittel erhöhen.	The advertising campaign planned for next spring can only be started if you increase next year's advertising budget by a third.
7. Angesichts des geringen Umsatzes halten wir es für das Beste, den Vertretungsvertrag nicht zu verlängern.	In view of the poor turnover we think it best not to prolong the agency agreement.

D | Avoiding common mistakes

Wrong	Correct
1. We would like to invite you ~~to~~ a visit ~~on~~ our stand ~~on~~ the Boat Fair.	1. We would like to invite you **for** a visit **to** our stand **at** the Boat Fair.
2. We have learned ~~of~~ your website that you are looking for an agent.	2. We have learned **from** your website that you are looking for an agent.
3. We herewith appoint ~~you as sole agent~~ for our products.	3. We herewith appoint **you sole agent** for our products.
4. As our products are selling ~~good~~ in your country …	4. As our products are selling **well** in your country …
5. You will be granted a ~~provision~~ of 12%.	5. You will be granted a **commission** of 12%.
6. The agreement is to be terminated ~~from~~ 31 December.	6. The agreement is to be terminated **as of** 31 December.

16

Job applications

A | Introduction

More and more people are taking advantage of the free movement of labour within the EU, i.e. their right to look for a job in another EU country and take up residence there. Apart from ease of
5 travel this is one of the most practical advantages of the EU for the ordinary citizen. Many apply for jobs in Britain as well educated Europeans usually have a good level of competence in English. Setting up a company there is often easier with
10 fewer bureaucratic hurdles involved. Immigration makes for a more efficient and generally younger workforce but the downside is that high levels of immigration may put considerable additional pressure on social services, education and housing.
15 There are various ways of finding out what vacancies exist. Many firms advertise openings in the newspapers, in Britain often on different days for specific professions. Apart from government-funded Job Centres, there are also job exchanges on the in-
20 ternet which specialise in many different positions. All major newspapers also have jobs websites. Alternatively, you can simply type your qualification/job title into a search engine, which will give you more specialist websites – for example hotel
25 jobs, jobs in insurance, freight forwarding, etc. This is particularly convenient if you are applying from abroad, as it obviates the necessity of buying expensive newspapers and periodicals which may not be readily available. It is also possible to look for
30 a position through a specialist recruitment agency (e. g. nurses, carers). If there are not enough positions advertised in a given field people often send unsolicited applications to organisations which are likely to need to recruit staff. It is also important
35 to realise that the titles of jobs advertised may not correspond exactly to your qualifications.
When applying in English – and there are an increasing number of international companies in continental Europe whose company language is
40 English – it is important to be aware of differences. Do not send references if applying in Britain. A potential employer will ask you to give the names of referees and will then approach them direct to obtain a reference. It is as well to warn people in
45 advance if you plan to give their names as referees! Do not include a photograph in your CV. You should make no reference to your parents' profession. A modern CV often reverses the chronological order and starts with the most recent
50 information on your career before giving details of previous employment, training and educational qualifications. A good CV needs to do two things – it needs to give the necessary information about qualifications, skills, experience, etc. – and it must

55 seek to PERSUADE (without exaggeration or embroidering on the truth!). A recent article with statements by major recruiters emphasises the following main points:

– focus on your skills
60 – tell the truth

– try to stand out from the crowd
– use a layout with "easy on the eye" spacing
– use language sparingly, avoid flowery prose ("Recruiters who have to plough through
65 hundreds of CVs don't enjoy flowery prose!")
– use active verbs and bullet points

B | Model application letter, CV and job interview

1 Application letter (structure)

Michael Reuter
91056 Erfurt
Klostergasse 37
Germany
Tel.: +49 (0)361 21 15 51...
E-mail: mreuter@aol... .com

23 April 201_   date

Jonathan Keeley
Southlands Nanosystems
72 Wivelsfield Rd
Chichester
PO18 6DN
UK

address and name of person to contact, where given

Dear Mr Keeley

I saw your advertisement for a systems administrator on the website of the London Evening Standard and should like to apply for this position.   say where you saw the ad

After completing my education at the Higher Commercial College in Suhl I did a 3-year traineeship with the company Angersoftware Gmbh, a small but dynamic company with 20 employees in Erfurt, Germany.   state qualifications

Since 2011 I have been working with Angersoftware GmbH as a junior systems administrator. I now have considerable experience both of software systems and helping to run a busy office. I feel well qualified for the position advertised.   give details of experience

I have a good command of English. I had 7 years of English at school and during my traineeship I prepared for and passed a state examination in English for commercial and administrative professions. I also have a working knowledge of French.   mention other qualifications

I enclose my CV and certified translations of my certificates. I should be pleased to provide names of referees if required.   send CV and copies of certificates, mention referees

I look forward to hearing from you. I would very much enjoy the challenge of working for a company in Britain.   concluding remarks

Yours sincerely

Michael Reuter
Enclosures

2 CV (German/English)

Persönliche Angaben

Name	Michael Reuter
Adresse	91056 Erfurt
	Klostergasse 37
	Tel. 0361–21 15 51...
	E-Mail: mreuter@aol... .com
Staatsangehörigkeit	deutsch
Geburtstag	18.08.1992
Geburtsort	98693 Ilmenau
Familienstand	ledig

Schulbildung

2008 – 2010	Höhere Handelsschule, BIZ Berufsbildungszentrum, Suhl
2006 – 2008	Goethe-Gymnasium Ilmenau
	Abschluss: Fachhochschulreife
2002 – 2006	Lindenberg-Realschule, Ilmenau
	Abschluss: Fachoberschulreife
1998 – 2002	Grundschule Am Kickelhahn, Ilmenau

Ausbildung

2011 – 2014	Ausbildung zum Informatikkaufmann bei Angersoftware GmbH, Erfurt
Mai 2014	Abschlussprüfung, Note: gut
2013	Zertifikatsprüfung Englisch für kaufmännische und verwaltende Berufe, Niveau I

Tätigkeiten

2014 – heute	Junior Systemadministrator bei Angersoftware GmbH, Erfurt

Tätigkeitsschwerpunkte:

2nd Level Support:	Benutzerbetreuung
	Behebung von Hard- und Softwarefehlern
Serverbetreuung:	Serverinstallation und -wartung
	Benutzerverwaltung
	Benutzerberechtigungen

2010 – 2011	FSJ (Freiwilliges Soziales Jahr) in einem Altenheim
Juli/August 2008	Praktikum bei Computer-Service Kienast, Ilmenau

Sonstige Kenntnisse

MCSE Zertifizierung
Office Programme
Englisch fließend, Französisch ausbaufähig

Interessen

Fitness, Marathon, Entwicklung von Computerspielen

Personal details:

Name:	Michael Reuter
Address:	91056 Erfurt
	Klostergasse 37
	Tel. +49 361 211551...
	E-mail: mreuter@aol... .com

Nationality:	German
Date of birth:	18 August 1992
Place of birth:	986935 Ilmenau, Germany
Marital status:	single

Present position:

2014 – present

Junior systems administrator at Angersoftware GmbH, Erfurt
Main fields:
2nd level support:
– user support
– resolution of hardware and software defects

Server support:
– server installation and maintenance
– user administration
– user privileges

Vocational training:

2011 – 2014	Traineeship as IT Consultant with Angersoftware GmbH, Erfurt
May 2014	Final examination and grade: good (= B)
2013	State certificate: English for commercial and administrative professions, Level I

Educational background:

2008 – 2010	Höhere Handelsschule (higher commercial college), Berufsbildungszentrum (centre of vocational training), Suhl
2006 – 2008	Goethe-Gymnasium (grammar school) Ilmenau
	School Leaving Certificate (examination enabling student to enrol at a polytechnic university)
2002 – 2006	Lindenberg Realschule (technical secondary school), Ilmenau
	School leaving certificate enabling student to continue education at a higher vocational college.
1998 – 2002	Grundschule (primary school) Am Kickelhahn, Ilmenau

Additional Skills:

MCSE certification
Office programmes
Fluent English, working knowledge of French

Additional Experience:

2010 – 2011	Voluntary social service in an old people's home
July – August 2008	Practical at Computer-Service Kienast, Ilmenau

Interests:

Fitness, marathons, designing computer games

3 Job interview

Trent Ceramics Ltd, a highly successful manufacturer of designer tiles, are looking to recruit a German and French speaking export assistant to join their team on a permanent basis. They have shortlisted a number of applicants and have decided to interview Martina Helbig.

MD: Good morning, Martina – I'm Madeleine Davies, head of HR here at Trent Ceramics. I see from your application that you were born in Germany but have been working in the UK for a couple of years.

MH: Yes, I always wanted to move to Britain and am happy in my present job but unfortunately it doesn't give me any opportunity to use my German or French.

MD: How fluent is your French?

MH: I spent 6 months in France when I was 18 and worked for a French company in Lyon for about a year after I finished my training as an export assistant in Germany. So it's very fluent and I'm familiar with all the commercial terms in French.

MD: Excellent. You would have a lot of contact with our customers in Germany, Austria and France. We also have agents in these countries who we are in regular contact with.
You may also be responsible for customers outside the EU. How familiar are you with export documentation?

MH: My training covered export documentation and means of payment in foreign trade and I was dealing with this on a daily basis at the French company.

MD: Good. You would be part of a small team here but a lot of the time you would be working independently. How would you feel about that?

MH: That's what I enjoyed about my job at the French firm. It was a small company and I had a lot of responsibility and was working on my own a lot of the time.

MD: What do you know about our company?

MH: I researched it on the internet and looked at your website.
I know it was founded almost two hundred years ago – one of the potteries around Stoke-on-Trent. I've also seen your tiles with their beautiful colour range and glazes.

MD: Excellent. How soon would you be able to start?

MH: Well, I'd have to give notice in my present job but I think I could start in two to three months' time at the latest.

MD: That would be OK. Is there anything you'd like to ask me?

MH: Your ad gave the starting salary at £25,000 p.a. Is that what I would be earning?

MD: Yes that would be your starting salary – here's a leaflet giving you details of other benefits – the pension scheme, for instance, and we have very good catering arrangements for our staff.

MH: Thank you.

MD: We'll be in touch with you within two weeks from today. Thank you very much for coming to this interview. Goodbye, Martina

MH: Thank you. Goodbye.

C | Tool kit

1 Phrases: Application

To refer to the source of address

I saw your advertisement in ...

I saw this vacancy advertised on the ... website.

I should like to apply for the position advertised in the ...

I have been given your address by ... who told me that you have a vacancy for ...

I am applying on the off-chance that you may have a vacancy.

To give reasons for applying

I am particularly attracted to this position as ...

I have just completed a traineeship at ...

I completed an apprenticeship two years ago.

I have some experience in the export trade.

I am familiar with this kind of work.

I am used to working with people.

I enjoy working with people.

I enjoy working in a team.

I would welcome the opportunity to ...

I am keen to use my knowledge of English and French.

To refer to certificates and references

I enclose certified copies of my certificates ...

I enclose certified translations of ...

I should be happy to provide the names of referees.

To refer to qualifications

I have good admin and bookkeeping skills.

I have completed an apprenticeship in ...

I took my Abitur two years ago.

My main subjects included English and Maths.

I have trained as a ...

I have considerable experience in ...

I spent two months in St Albans on a placement.

I have done a practical with a small travel operator /a freight forwarder/an export-import firm/a wholesaler.

I did my apprenticeship with the ... company.

To refer to starting date and relocation

I would be able to start at short notice.

I would have to give the usual notice at my present firm.

I could start on 1 August.

I would be prepared to move to ...

To close the letter

I look forward to hearing from you ...

I hope that you consider my application suitable and give me the opportunity to present myself at an interview.

Communication across cultures: Paraphrasing German job titles

While the German *duales Bildungssystem* has been much admired, it is also criticised for its rigidity. Thus, the many job titles in Germany involving a particular type of training (e.g.
5 apprenticeship) and an examination before the *Industrie- und Handelskammer* or the *Handwerks-kammer* often have no direct equivalent in English and advertisements for these jobs simply do not exist in British newspapers or on
10 websites. It is important to look carefully at the job description and consider whether the skills required are covered by your qualifications and experience. In more technical or traditional professions (especially those involving danger)
15 such as electricians, plumbers or central heating installers there is a tradition of apprenticeships very similar to that in Germany.

Otherwise more general, transferable skills are emphasised rather than narrowly defined
20 professions. German professions such as *Fremdsprachenkorrespondent/in, Kaufmann/-frau für Büromanagement, Fremdsprachensekretär/in, Wirtschaftsassistent/in,* possibly even *Hotelkauf-mann/-frau* might all be subsumed under the
25 heading of secretary (with foreign languages). The word secretary or PA covers a wide variety of positions. Successful PA/administrators with proven abilities and experience often command high salaries. Initial training may be briefer
30 than in Germany with additional qualifications added later. Paraphrasing *"Kaufmann/-frau"* is a major problem: the word "clerk" is used in banking, insurance and the freight forwarding business. If you are looking for jobs on the
35 internet type in "insurance clerk", for example. The expression "management assistant" is also recommended by the umbrella organisation of German chambers of commerce as a paraphrase. However, if you type in "management assistant"
40 on the internet you will get "assistant manager" jobs which will require several years' experience in a management role. You will probably not find the jobs you are looking for.

The aim when trying to translate a German job
45 title must be to paraphrase it in English in such a way that a potential employer in Britain (or in any other EU-country) has a realistic impression of the skills and experience of an applicant. There is no point in giving yourself an
50 impressive sounding title if you are deflated at your job interview. English books on making applications frequently emphasise the need for realism and truthfulness.

2 Job titles (German/English)

1. Kaufmann/-frau für Tourismus und Freizeit	a. tourism and leisure consultant
2. Einzelhandelskaufmann/-frau	b. retail management assistant
3. Fremdsprachensekretär/in	c. secretary with foreign languages
4. Kaufmann/-frau für Spedition und Logistikdienstleistung	d. freight forwarding and logistics assistant/clerk
5. Veranstaltungskaufmann/-frau	e. assistant events coordinator
6. Industriekaufmann/-frau	f. industrial clerk
7. Automobilkaufmann/-frau	g. car sales management assistant
8. Kaufmann/-frau für Büromanagement	h. office administration assistant
9. Werbekaufmann/-frau	i. advertising assistant
10. Groß- und Außenhandelskaufmann/-frau	j. wholesale and export assistant
11. Versicherungskaufmann/-frau	k. insurance clerk
12. Informatikkaufmann/-frau	l. IT consultant
13. Verlagskaufmann/-frau	m. publisher's assistant
14. Bankkaufmann/-frau	n. banking clerk

Socializing in a business environment

A | Introduction

There is a saying in the German language which sums up rather neatly the cultural differences that exist between Germany and the English-speaking world when it comes to national attitudes towards work and private life – "Dienst ist Dienst, und Schnaps ist Schnaps". This phrase indicates that Germans – and Austrians, or Swiss for that matter – draw a clear line between private and professional spheres. Most work from 9 till 5, and then go home to enjoy their family life, their circle of friends or whatever their choice regarding the organisation of their spare time may be.

Things are slightly different in Anglo-Saxon business culture. The two spheres tend to overlap, are more intertwined and the boundaries are often blurred. People take work home with them, meet up with colleagues outside office hours and are expected to work beyond the 5 pm watershed if there are urgent matters to be dealt with.
This may sound familiar to some employees in the German-speaking world, but the intermingling of the two spheres goes even further. Company dos, fundraising events, outings and similar semi-private occasions introduce an element of informality into business life.
This informality finds its expression in the way matters are discussed and people talk to each other. Before you get down to business, whether you talk to someone in person or over the phone, you usually have a brief chat about

personal matters or, say, the weather. Even when discussing business matters, the tone is usually much more personal than in Germany and people are generally on first-name terms.

When hosting business meetings, the British, for instance, tend to try and introduce an element of pleasurable sociability so that the dividing line between business and pleasure may be less easy to see.

Dress codes are probably even stricter than in Germany, and dressing smartly is the rule.

The fact that you will often be in contact with colleagues in a non-business context requires some knowledge regarding conventions in private or semi-private communication, be it written or oral.

In this chapter we will be looking at some typical situations such as private invitations and congratulations that you may be confronted with when working in an English-speaking environment.

B | Model dialogue/e-mail/letter

1 Model dialogue: The company "do" and private events

> ⓘ **INFO: A company do**
>
> A "do" can be any sort of private or semi-private event, ranging from the office Christmas party and the celebration of someone's promotion or retirement to a fundraising event. The latter is quite common in English-speaking countries where the proceeds of ticket sales – be they dinner tickets or lottery tickets – as well as any donations made are given to a charitable organisation.

Petra Schneider is on an internship with a British company at the moment. She receives a call from her colleague Martin Cook:

PS: Good morning, Petra Schneider speaking.

MC: Hi Petra. This is Martin from the office. How's it going?

PS: Oh, hi Martin. I'm good, thanks. You?

MC: Yah, not too bad. Listen Petra, the reason I'm calling is our do next Wednesday evening. Has Charlene given you any information yet?

PS: Er ... no. I was out of the office most of last week. I was up in London.

MC: Oh, yes, of course. Now, you may have heard about the disastrous floods in Somerset last month.

PS: Yes, I have. Horrific, isn't it? So many people have lost their belongings and can't move back into their homes.

MC: Exactly. That's why Charlene thought it would be a brilliant idea to organise a fundraising event for the families who are worst affected.

PS: That sounds like an excellent idea. How are you going to organise it?

MC: Here's the plan: Charlene thinks we should all bring along something home-made. You know, like a salad, a cake or some sort of pudding, or maybe a roast if you're up for that. Anyway, something to eat or drink. If you're not such a brilliant cook, bring a couple of bottles of wine. Then we're all going to invite friends and family. We'll put the food and drinks on a large buffet table and people can buy meal and drinks tickets. All the proceeds will be given to those families in Somerset.

PS: That sounds great, but the office is much too small for that.

MC: Well, yes of course. Do you know the Green Dragon?

PS: The large pub near the station?

MC: Exactly. They have a large function room that they let for free.

PS: Excellent. How many people do you expect will come?

MC: Well, we're twelve at the office, including you. If everybody's going to bring, say, 3 or 4 friends that would make it roughly 50 people or so.

PS: What about the music?

MC: I'll organise all that. A friend of mine is in a sort of folk band. They would be happy to do a gig that evening. And then, of course, there's the pub's sound system. I'll just bring along my tablet with all my music and we'll take it from there. So, what do you say?

PS: I think it's a brilliant idea. I could make a nice big bowl of salad and invite my friends Lisa and Robert. Oh, and perhaps my neighbour Annabel. She's a very nice woman.

MC: Good! I'm glad you're going to join us. Are you back in the office on Monday?

PS: Yes, I'll have to work on the Huberling files.

MC: Any plans for the weekend?

PS: Not really. I think I'll just relax. London has quite exhausted me.

MC: I bet. It always does. Well, just take it easy and chill out over the weekend.

PS: Will do, Martin. Good to hear from you and thanks for letting me know about the do.

MC: See you Monday then. Take care. Bye.

PS: Bye.

> ⓘ **INFO: Abbreviations**
>
> Abbreviations are quite common when modern media such as PCs and smartphones are used. This is particularly true of less formal communication. However, as pointed out in the section on formal and informal language, modern predictive software makes the use of many abbreviations superfluous. Besides, the overuse of abbreviations may be regarded as a sign that you don't take your time to respond to a message or email and that it is too much of an effort for you to spell out a word or expression. And this, of course, may imply that your communication partner is not important to you. In other words, too many abbreviations may come across as inconsiderate.
>
> However, there are some standard abbreviations that have become acceptable both in formal and informal contexts and that you should be aware of:
>
> | | |
> |---|---|
> | fyi | for your information |
> | asap | as soon as possible |
> | rsvp | please reply (from the French "repondez s'il vous plait"). This is quite common in invitations. |
> | w/c | week commencing (=beginning) |
> | p/a | per annum (per year) |
> | tba | to be announced |
> | imo | in my opinion |

Please avoid abbreviations that you could quite easily spell out, such as "thx" (thanks), "pls" (please) or "l8r" (later). You should also avoid abbreviations that you may find quite often in social media, but which may be regarded as inappropriate in a business context (even in a semi-private situation). These include "lol" (laugh out loud), "myob" (mind you own business) or "wtf" (we're not going to explain that one – lol!). An "x" at the end of a text message or email stands for "kiss". Think twice before using it!

Don't worry too much about whether to use upper or lower case, punctuation or no punctuation when using the above list of abbreviations. ASAP is just as good as asap, and tba and t.b.a. are both fine. Remember that German speakers take these formalities much more seriously than English speakers.

2 E-mail: Announcing an office get-together

⊗ ⊖ ⊕

...

Dear all,

Most of you will be aware that at the end of this month Deirdre will be leaving our company for pastures new*.

I thought it would be nice to have a get-together in our main meeting room on Tuesday during lunch break. Snacks and drinks will be provided.

It would be great if you could contribute to a nice farewell present. There is an envelope for that purpose in Lorna's office. I've also left a card with Lorna, and it would be great if you could sign it and add some good wishes or whatever message you want to leave for Deirdre.

The get-together is to be a surprise so please don't mention anything to Deirdre when you see her.

Hope to see you all on Tuesday.

Janet

*a new area of activities

3 Letter: Written invitation

Dear Peter

Sarah and Chris are getting married and would love to see you at their wedding service at St. Bartholomew's, Brighton, on 6 September 201_ at 11 am.
After the service there will be a celebration at nearby Duke's Arms Hotel in Hanover Crescent to which you are cordially invited.

Dress code: smart-casual
RSVP

Sarah Vaughan

Chris Merton

3.1 Letter: Accepting an invitation

Dear Sarah, dear Chris,

Thank you very much for the invitation to your wedding service and the celebration at the Duke's Arms.
I shall be delighted to come and look forward very much to seeing you both on 6 September.

All the best

Peter Meyerling

3.2 Letter: Declining an invitation

Dear Sarah and Chris

Thank you so much for the kind invitation to your wedding celebration.
Unfortunately, I will not be able to celebrate with you as I will be at an important business convention in Dublin on that day.
I wish you all the very best and hope to see you soon in Brighton.

Best wishes

Hannelore Sichelschmidt

4 Letter: Congratulations

Dear Mitch,

I was delighted to hear about your promotion to Chief Financial Officer at your company.
I wish you all the very best and much success in your new job and look forward to seeing you soon in Essen.

Kind regards

Jonathan Bauer

5 Letter: Condolence

Dear Mary

It is with great sadness that we learnt about the death of your husband.
William was a great friend and business partner and will be sorely missed by
all of us.
On behalf of Meier GmbH I would ask you to accept the expression of our
deepest sympathy.

Yours very truly

Karl Leutner

C | Tool kit

Building blocks

As most of the situations dealt with in this chapter are semi-private, the
language used may be less formulaic and more individual. There are,
nevertheless, building blocks for written communication which are useful in
such situations as expressing congratulations or condolences. There are also
some useful building blocks in Unit 4 (Making arrangements).

Congratulations

I/we would like to congratulate you on	your promotion/your new job.
Congratulations on	the birth of your daughter.
I was/we were delighted/thrilled to hear about	your new house.

I/we wish you all the (very) best for	
All the (very) best for	your new career
I/we wish you much success with	your new company
I/we wish you much success in	your new job/position
With our best wishes for	

Holidays

Sending Christmas cards is more common in the English-speaking world (while
birthday greetings are less common and less formal than in Germany). If, for
whatever reason, you wish to avoid religious allusions in your greetings, there
are many different options (see box below). Please be aware that your business
friends may be Muslim, Jewish or Hindu. So it might be a nice gesture to send
greetings on the occasion of Eid, Hanukkah or Diwali. You will have to find out
when these important festivals take place in a given year as they are movable
feasts.

Merry Christmas and a Happy New Year!
Happy holidays and much success in the New Year!
I/we wish you a very happy Christmas and a successful New Year.
Enjoy the Christmas holidays and have a happy and successful New Year.
Have a good holiday and a great 201_.

Condolence

We were very sad to learn about	the death of your …
It is with great sadness that we learned about	the passing of your …

The news that your …. died/passed away last … came as a great shock.
Please accept the expression of our sincerest/deepest sympathy.

 INFO: Colloquial language

As we've already pointed out in the Introduction to this chapter, the language you will be confronted with in an Anglo-Saxon business environment will in all probability be less formal than that used in German-speaking countries in a similar context. The degree of formality decreases even further of course once you leave the office and find yourself in a private or semi-private environment with your English-speaking colleagues or business partners.

But be wary of the many potential pitfalls! As a non-native speaker you will not have the natural feeling for what is adequate and acceptable. Colloquialisms and slang expressions vary widely geographically (what may be acceptable in, say, Australia may be regarded as rude in Canada or the other way round). Besides, colloquial language changes much more quickly than more conservative informal structures. Words or expressions come and go and their meanings undergo subtle or even radical changes over time. An example is the word "wicked" which, originally, refers to a deed, person or trait of character that is regarded as evil and malicious. Roughly 15 years ago, it entered the world of youth-speak as an expression denoting the exact opposite – "that's so wicked", you could hear young people say when they talked about something they found very "cool". This use has by now probably gone out of fashion and the word has returned to its original meaning.

So if you want to avoid sounding hopelessly old-fashioned or, even worse, cause embarrassment, misunderstandings or offence, you should play the safe card and avoid colloquialisms. Unless, that is, you are 100% sure that the expression used is still current and acceptable.

Anhang

1 | Memos and reports

1.1 Memos

Memos are a form of communication between people working in the same company. Nowadays in large companies they are often sent by e-mail via the company intranet.

5 Where they are written in the traditional way, companies often have their own printed memo forms. Whatever the actual design of these forms, it is necessary to give:

- · the name of the sender
- 10 · the name of the recipient
- · the date and time
- · the subject

The form will generally look like this:

Heading

From:
To:
Date + time:
Subject:

15 The subject matter should be explained briefly and concisely. You should make sure that any names, dates, phone numbers, e-mail addresses, figures etc. are given accurately. A paper memo may be initialled but unlike 20 letters it does not have a complimentary close.

2.2 Reports

Reports generally contain more information than a brief memo. Often research on some level to collate the relevant data is necessary to produce a report.

5 Reports may be **informal** if they are intended for one person or for distribution within the company. The report should have a heading, give the name and position of the author and show the date when it was written.

10 A more **formal** format is required if the report is destined for a wider public, i.e. for distribution outside the company. It should have a title page giving

- · the title of the report
- 15 · the name and position of the addressee (if it is intended for an individual)

- · the name and position of the author
- · the date of production

The report should have a clear structure with 20 headings to highlight the different sections and various aspects of the subject matter.

Example:
Georg Roth of Comestas-Gourmet GmbH is concerned that sales to Portugal have slumped 25 *due to the recession. He asks his assistant to prepare a 2-3 page report giving statistics and an analysis of sales in the year to date. The report is intended for his personal consumption so will not be circulated.*

2 | Incoterms 2010

The Incoterms rules describe the tasks, costs and risks involved in the delivery of goods from the seller to the buyer. Reference to an Incoterms 2010 rule in a sales contract clearly defines the parties'
5 respective obligations and reduces the risk of legal complications. Trade blocs, like the EU, having made border formalities less significant, the Incoterms 2010 can be applied in both international and domestic sale contracts.

10 Since their creation by the International Chamber of Commerce (ICC) in Paris in 1936 the Incoterms have regularly been updated. The latest update, Incoterms 2010, takes account of the continued spread of customs-free zones, the increased use of
15 electronic communications (electronic documents), the heightened concern about security and the changes in transport practices (containerisation).

The Incoterms 2010 reduce the total number of rules from 13 to 11:

20 – The new rule DAT (Delivered at Terminal), under which the goods are placed at the buyer's disposal unloaded from the arriving vehicle, replaces the former DEQ rule.

– The new rule DAP (Delivered at Place), under
25 which the goods are placed at the buyer's disposal ready for unloading, replaces the former rules DAF, DES and DDU.

The 11 Incoterms 2010 rules are presented in two distinct classes:

30 – Seven Incoterms (EXW, FCA, CPT, CIP, DAT, DAP, DDP) that can be used irrespective of the mode of transport and irrespective of whether one or more modes of transport are employed. These rules can also be used in cases where a ship is
35 used for part of the carriage.

– Four Incoterms (FAS, FOB, CFR, CIF) where both the place where the risk passes from the seller to the buyer and the place of destination are ports. Under the last three Incoterms rules the "ship's
40 rail" as the point where the risk passes from the seller to the buyer has been replaced by "on board" the vessel.

Under all Incoterms clauses the seller must deliver the goods to the buyer at the named place/port
45 and the buyer must take delivery of the goods. The seller must procure or help to procure the transport documents and pack the goods, if customary.

Note that under the Incoterms CPT, CIP, CFR and CIF the seller bears the risks only up to the place where
50 the goods are handed over to the (first) carrier or on board ship in the port of shipment, respectively. Under these terms the seller must, however, contract and pay for the carriage to the place or port of destination.

nach ICC Incoterms 2010 © 2010 International Chamber of Commerce (ICC) Incoterms® 2010 Rules by the International Chamber of Commerce

Business basics: Incoterms 2010		
Rules for any mode or modes of transport	**EXW**	Ex Works (… named place of delivery)
	FCA	Free Carrier (… named place of delivery)
	CPT	Carriage paid to (… named place of destination)
	CIP	Carriage and Insurance paid to (… named place of destination)
	DAT	Delivered at Terminal (… named terminal at port or place of destination)
	DAP	Delivered at Place (… named place of destination)
	DDP	Delivered Duty paid (… named place of destination)
Rules for sea and inland waterway transport	**FAS**	Free alongside Ship (… named port of shipment)
	FOB	Free on Board (… named port of shipment)
	CFR	Cost and Freight (… named port of destination)
	CIF	Cost, Insurance and Freight (… named port of destination)

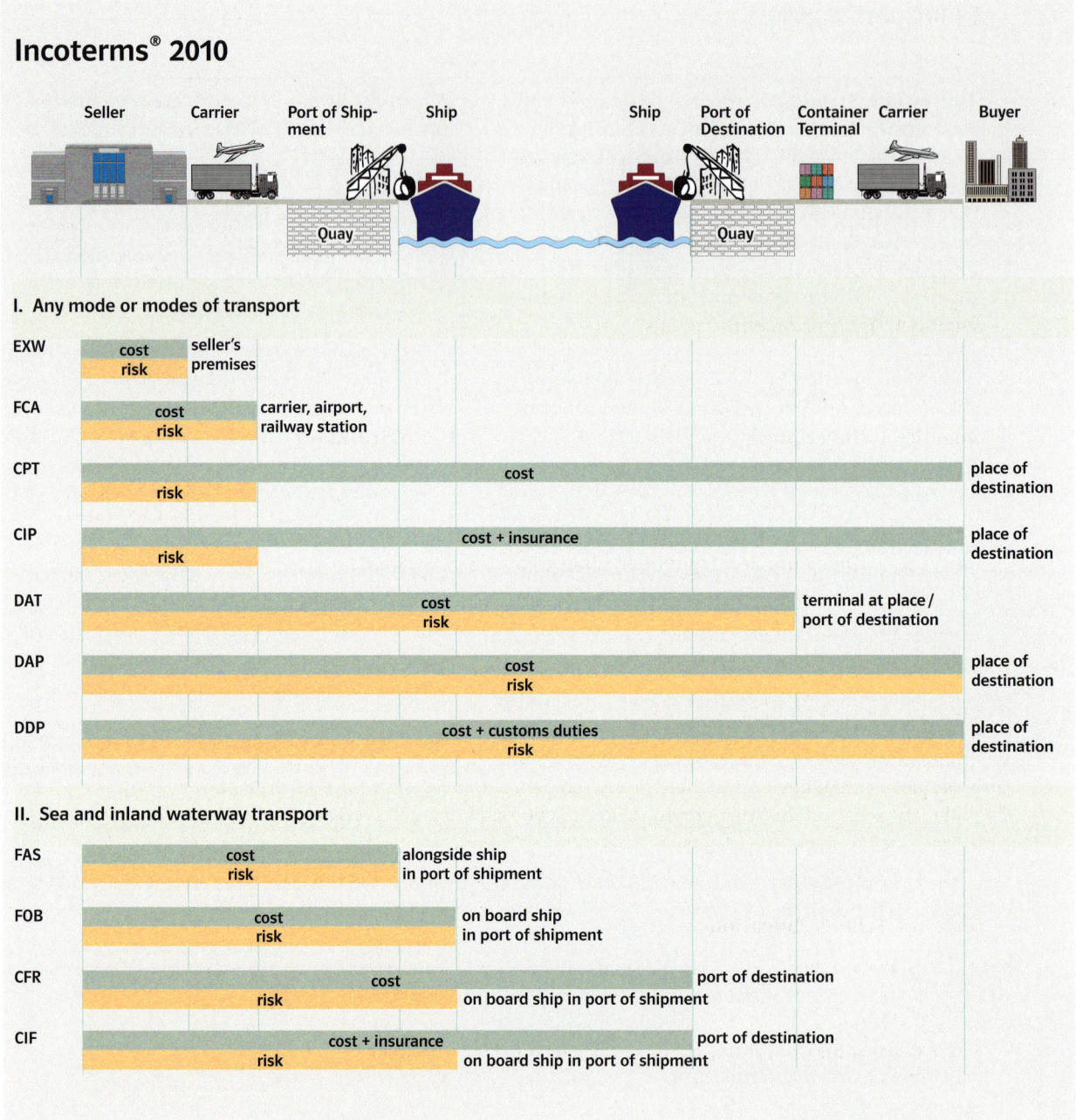

Incoterms® 2010

| | Seller | Carrier | Port of Shipment | Ship | | Ship | Port of Destination | Container Terminal | Carrier | Buyer |

I. Any mode or modes of transport

EXW — cost / risk — seller's premises

FCA — cost / risk — carrier, airport, railway station

CPT — cost / risk — place of destination

CIP — cost + insurance / risk — place of destination

DAT — cost / risk — terminal at place / port of destination

DAP — cost / risk — place of destination

DDP — cost + customs duties / risk — place of destination

II. Sea and inland waterway transport

FAS — cost / risk — alongside ship in port of shipment

FOB — cost / risk — on board ship in port of shipment

CFR — cost / risk — port of destination / on board ship in port of shipment

CIF — cost + insurance / risk — port of destination / on board ship in port of shipment

nach Incoterms® 2010 © International Chamber of Commerce, (ICC)

3 | Sales contract

CONTRACT FOR THE SALE OF GOODS

Section 1: Identities of the parties

Ergo Bueromoebel GmbH, An der Iller 44–46, 87509 Immenstadt, Germany, hereinafter referred to as Seller and Meximétrico S.A., Av. Insurgentes 311, 11560 Mexico D.F., Mexico, hereinafter referred to as Buyer, hereby agree to the following terms.

Section 2: Description of the goods

Seller agrees to transfer and deliver to Buyer, on or before 30 September 201_, the goods described below:

Quantity	Description	Unit Price (Euro)
200	Ergonomic Office Chair OFM-241	135.50
200	Ergonomic Task Chair OFM-312	145.20
200	Conference Chair OCM-306	185.50
100	Dual Function Ergonomic Chair OFM-220	285.20
100	Leather Executive Chair OEM-56	395.50
200	Visitor Chair OVM-604	115.20
	less 10 % quantity discount	

Section 3: Buyer's rights and obligations

Buyer agrees to accept the goods and pay for them by irrevocable documentary letter of credit to be opened with Banco Internacional, Mexico D.F., in favour of the Seller. Under the terms of delivery agreed upon the goods are deemed received by the Buyer on passing the ship's rail at the port of shipment. Buyer reserves the right to cancel the order if delivery is not effected by the aforemen-tioned date.

Section 4: Seller's obligations

Seller delivers the goods FOB the vessel named by the Buyer at the port of shipment. Seller warrants these products to be free of defects in material and workmanship for a period of 36 months. If the products show any defects within the warranty period, Seller shall, at his discretion, either replace or repair the product.

Section 5: Attestation

Agreed to on this 20th day of August, in the year 201_

By:

Carmen Martinez

(Carmen Martinez), Head Buyer
on behalf of Meximétrico S.A., Buyer
Seller

By:

Jochen Hoffmann

(Jochen Hoffmann), Export Manager
On behalf of Ergo Bueromoebel GmbH,

4 | Negotiations

4.1 Negotiations Dos and Don'ts

– Prepare all the necessary material beforehand and make sure you have it at your fingertips. Define your aims.
– Go through the different scenarios (What should I say if they ...).
– Expect the unexpected.
– Knowing the strengths and weaknesses of your competitors' products or services is also important.
– Work out your strategy beforehand. Have a fall-back position if it becomes apparent that you are not going to fully achieve an aim.
– Decide what your bottom line is, i.e. the minimum you need to achieve.
– Do not reveal your bargaining position at the outset as this reduces your scope of flexibility. However, avoid conceding too much too quickly.
– Empathise with the other side. Try to find out what he/she expects/wants/ needs. Where possible create a feeling that you are partners rather than opponents.
– Avoid direct questions that might seem impertinent or invasive. There are cultural differences in the degree of directness which is considered acceptable.
– Do not underestimate your opposite number. Whatever his negotiating style you can be sure he will have done his homework.
– Watch out for possibilities of compromise or trade-offs – i.e. conceding something in order to get something in return.
– Remember that your opposite number will also need to feel that he's got a good deal.
– Finalise the agreement. Summarize verbally and/or follow up with a written summary. Make sure that everyone has the same perspective on what has been agreed (it is often surprising how much perceptions of the same situation may differ).

4.2 Communication across cultures: Negotiating

Negotiating, like any other form of communication, is profoundly influenced by culture. Culture dictates what is felt to be appropriate behaviour. Successful negotiating in a cross-cultural context
5 involves being aware of all the factors that may influence the outcome. Does eye contact convey confidence and sincerity or might it be seen as impolite or intrusive? Is it essential to establish a friendly and trusting relationship between the
10 negotiating parties or are negotiations seen as purely function-al? How much small talk is expected (probably more in the UK than in Germany) and what topics are appropriate?
The physical distance between two people which is
15 instinctively felt to be normal differs from culture to culture. This may lead to a kind of dance where each tries to establish the distance or closeness felt to be normal. The amount of touching also differs. In Germany or Britain this is restricted to a hand-

20 shake during introductions. A hearty slap on the back, a hug or a complex system of kissing would probably not go down too well.

How should people be addressed? In English-speaking countries it is usual to give both first name and 25 surname when introducing yourself. After that, first names will generally be used. Academic titles (e.g. Dr) are used in Germany or Italy, for example, but only in an academic context in Britain. However, titles such as Lord or Sir are used.

30 Research shows that British speakers prefer less direct verbal strategies to express disagreement or reluctance than their German counterparts who tend to go for greater directness. Thus, "I agree with you up to a point, but…" may signal disagreement, 35 and "Do you really think so?" may mean "That cannot possibly be true." "I'm not entirely happy about this proposal" may indicate rejection. Thus, the possibilities for misunderstanding are clear. The German side may feel (wrongly) that resistance to 40 their proposals is minimal while the British may think that they have made their resistance quite clear.

As it is impossible to be prepared for all the cultural differences that exist, it is important to adopt 45 an investigative attitude, i.e. observe the other's behaviour sensitively and non-judgmentally.

5 | Cheques and banker's drafts

Cheques. The cheque has been a widespread and indispensable means of payment for many years. The first cheque was written some 350 years ago! However, cheques are being written less and less 5 frequently thanks to the widespread use of debit and credit cards to pay for groceries, clothes and other purchases. In the rapidly growing online retail sector apart from debit and credit cards payments are often made via PayPal, a global 10 e-commerce business which enables secure payments and money transfers to be made through the internet. At the same time, online banking makes it possible for individ-uals and companies to transfer money and pay bills electronically. 2018 is 15 the target year for phasing out cheques in the UK, though there is considerable resistance from those who see it as a useful way of paying the plumber or electrician.

Technically speaking, a cheque is an order in writ-20 ing made out by the holder of an account to his bank to pay a certain sum to a beneficiary. There are different types of cheque. Cheque books issued by banks in Britain contain only **crossed cheques**, which are the safest as they can only be paid into 25 the bank account of the payee nominated on the cheque. **Open cheques** are paid out in cash at the bank counter. **Bearer cheques** are literally payable to any bearer. They therefore carry considerable risk and are not much used. Finally, **order cheques** are 30 payable to a specified person or to his or her order. They are transferable by endorsement.

Banker's draft. A company (e.g. Riviera Fashions) wishing to purchase a quantity of goods worth £5,000 from another company with which it has not 35 had business relations (e.g. Strawberry Fair GmbH) may (if this is the means of payment agreed) ask its bank to issue a banker's draft – a cheque drawn by one bank on another made out to Strawberry Fair Ltd for the sum agreed and marked A/c payee. The 40 amount can only be credited to Strawberry Fair's account who can be sure of getting their money as the bank guarantees payment.

In the Eurozone payment by cheque is also likely to be phased out with the creation of SEPA, the Single 45 Euro Payments Area which has been extended to include EU member countries outside the Eurozone. The aim is to advance integration of the

Single Market by introducing more efficient and cheaper ways of making payments. Consumers and
50 companies in the Eurozone will not pay more for cross-border credit transfers, direct debits and card payments than for domestic transactions. The SEPA system also includes European Economic Area (EEA) countries Norway, Iceland, Liechtenstein, Monaco
55 and Switzerland. Changeover to the European

payment schemes for credit transfers and direct debits in euro took place in Februrary 2014. From then on national account numbers had to be
60 replaced by the International Bank Account Number (IBAN). Until 2016 the Bank Identifier Code (BIC), also called SWIFT code, will be required in cross-border transactions (see also Payment in Unit 9).

6 | Bills of exchange

According to the Bill of Exchange Act 1882, a bill of exchange is "an unconditional order in writing, addressed by one person to another, signed by the person giving it, requiring the person to whom
5 it is addressed to pay on demand or at a fixed or determinable future time a certain sum in money to, or to the order of, a specified person or to bearer."
There are three parties to a B/E: the **drawer** who
10 makes out the B/E, the **drawee** who is required to pay and the **payee** to whom the money is to be paid. Frequently, the payee is identical with the drawer. At its initial stage the B/E is called a **draft**.
A B/E has to be paid (honoured) either immediately,
15 i.e. at sight – then it is called a **sight draft** – or at a fixed or determinable future date, called the date of **maturity**. In this case it is called a **time bill**.

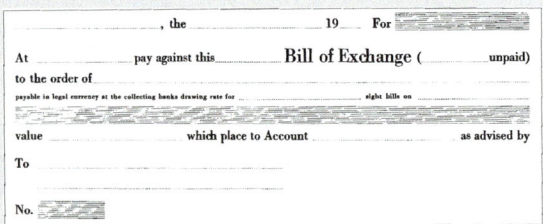

A time bill must be **accepted** by the drawee with his own signature on the face of the B/E and returned
20 to the drawer/payee. The B/E may then be referred to as an **acceptance**. The payee now has three options: he may

- keep the B/E until maturity
- pass it on to a creditor in payment
25 - have it discounted by a bank, which means that the bank will pay the face value of the B/E less a certain discount.

In the two latter cases the payee must endorse the B/E, i.e. sign it on the back (**endorsement**) in order
30 to transfer ownership of the B/E. Every holder of the B/E may, however, be held liable for payment if the B/E is not honoured at maturity. The B/E is of particular importance for business as it is both a means of payment and a means of credit. By
35 drawing a time bill on him, the drawer grants the drawee credit for the period until maturity while he himself may have the B/E discounted as soon as it has been accepted by the drawee. Thus the drawer (payee) may obtain the sum in question long before
40 the date of maturity.

How does the B/E work?

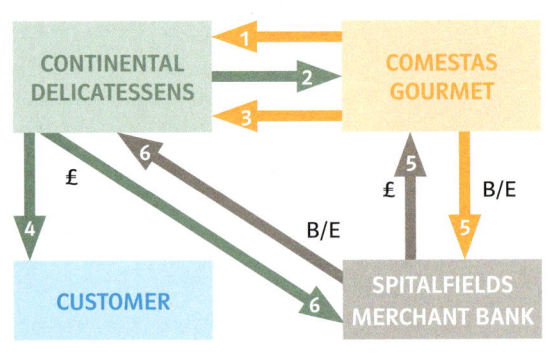

1. Comestas-Gourmet draws a B/E at 60 days on Continental Delicatessens. This means that Comestas-Gourmet requires Continental
45 Delicatessens to pay the amount of the B/E in 60 days and sends Continental Delicatessens the B/E for acceptance.
2. Continental Delicatessens accepts the B/E by signing it on the face. Thus Continental

50 Delicatessens confirms its obligation to pay. Continental Delicatessens then returns the accepted B/E to Comestas-Gourmet.

3. On receipt of the accepted B/E Comestas-Gourmet forwards the foodstuffs to Continental
55 Delicatessens.

4. Continental Delicatessens sells the foodstuffs to its customers.

5. Comestas-Gourmet endorses the B/E, i. e. signs it on the back, in order to have it discounted
50 by Spitalfields Merchant Bank. The bank pays Comestas-Gourmet the amount of the B/E less a small discount.

6. Two months later, Spitalfields Merchant Bank presents the B/E to Continental Delicatessens, and
55 Continental Delicatessens pays the full amount of the B/E to Spitalfields Merchant Bank.

Who benefits from the B/E?

1. The buyer, e. g. retailers such as Continental Delicatessens, who are granted credit until the

60 date of maturity if they accept a B/E. This enables Continental Delicatessens to sell the goods first and to honour the B/E afterwards out of the proceeds from the sale.

2. The seller, e. g. suppliers such as Comestas-
65 Gourmet, who are enabled to grant their customers credit by drawing a bill of exchange on them which is due at a later date. But Comestas-Gourmet need not wait for the money until then. Once the B/E has been accepted by Continental
70 Delicatessens, Comestas-Gourmet can have it discounted by a bank, e. g. Spitalfields Merchant Bank. That means Comestas-Gourmet receive the invoice amount (less the discount) long before the B/E is due for payment.

75 3. The bank, e. g. Spitalfields Merchant Bank, which is enabled to advance money and earns a certain percentage of the invoice amount by discounting the B/E.

7 | Types of firms and companies

A **sole trader** is the sole proprietor of a small business. Such businesses are mainly involved in the provision of services, e.g. small shops, hairdressing, IT services. Such firms can be set up with few legal
5 formalities and the owner can make independent decisions and retain all the profits. He or she is, however, fully liable, i. e. liable to the full extent of his or her personal fortune for any debts incurred by the firm.

10 A **partnership** is, according to the Partnership Act 1890, "the relation which subsists between persons carrying on a business in common with a view to profit". Partnerships are usual for firms of accountants, solicitors and doctors, etc. **Ordinary**
15 (or general) **partnerships** carry *unlimited liability* for all partners, with all partners taking part in the management of the firm. In a **limited partnership**, on the other hand, some partners are allowed *limited liability*. This means that their personal
20 assets (house, car, etc.) cannot be claimed by the partnership's creditors. The partnership is run by the ordinary partners who are fully liable for the obligations of the firm. In 2000 the **limited liability partnership (LLP)** was created. It is a legal person

25 separate from its members who all have limited liability.

Unlike the above-mentioned types of firm, **joint stock companies** (private limited companies and public limited companies) are incorporated, which
30 means that they are artificial legal entities that can conclude contracts, sue and be sued. They must be registered with the Registrar of Companies. *Shares* are sold to raise the capital for the company and the **shareholders**, i. e. the owners, enjoy limited
35 liability. The shareholders elect *a board of directors* who run the company on their behalf. Profits are

distributed to the owners in the form of *dividends*. In the United States such companies are called **corporations**.

40 **Private limited companies** may in many respects be compared with the German GmbH, but are not required to have a minimum share capital. They must use the abbreviation **Ltd** after their name. Their shares cannot be offered to the general 45 public and cannot, therefore, be traded at the stock exchange. There are certain requirements as far as the publication of accounts is concerned. Many former partnerships now prefer to operate as private limited companies. The US American equivalent is 50 the **closed corporation**, the legal form preferred for smaller and family-owned businesses.

Public limited companies are in many ways the British counterpart of the German AG. The latter is, however, run by two tiers of management, i. e. the 55 executive board (also called board of management) and the supervisory board, whereas, under English law, companies are run by one *board of directors* only, some of whom have executive functions while others play a supervisory role. Public limited 60 companies use the abbreviation **plc** (or PLC) after their names. They must have a minimum nominal share capital of £50,000 and their shares are often traded at the stock exchange. Their results must be published after presentation to the shareholders at 65 the *annual general meeting*. The distribution of profits in the form of dividends must also be approved by the shareholders at this meeting. The legal requirements are set out in the Companies Act 2006. In the United States similar companies are known as 70 **public/stock corporations** and account for 90 % of all turnover.

A **holding company** is formed for the special purpose of administering more than half of the share capital of one or more other companies, 75 called **subsidiaries**. A firm operating a business of its own while holding more than half of the shares of a subsidiary company is the latter's **parent company**.

Increasing 80 **globalisation** has accelerated the growth of big **multinational companies**, operating in many different countries. In order 85 to benefit from the advantages offered by specific locations, such as access to foreign markets, availability of 90 cheap labour, reduced transportation costs, government subsidies, softer regulations, tax 95 advantages, cheaper energy or raw materials and the like, major companies nowadays set up new companies in other countries or try to acquire existing companies. They do so either by means 100 of **mergers**, with both companies forming a new entity as equals, or by means of **take-overs**, where the stronger company takes control of the other, which stands to lose much of its identity. If a take-over is attempted against the wishes of the board 105 of directors and/or some of the shareholders of the company targeted, this is known as a *hostile* or unsolicited *take-over bid*.

8 | Organisation of companies

The larger a company is, the more complex its organisation tends to be. The scope of an individual employee's responsibilities will likewise be smaller and his or her duties more specialised in a large company than in a small one. Typically, a major company may be organised like this:

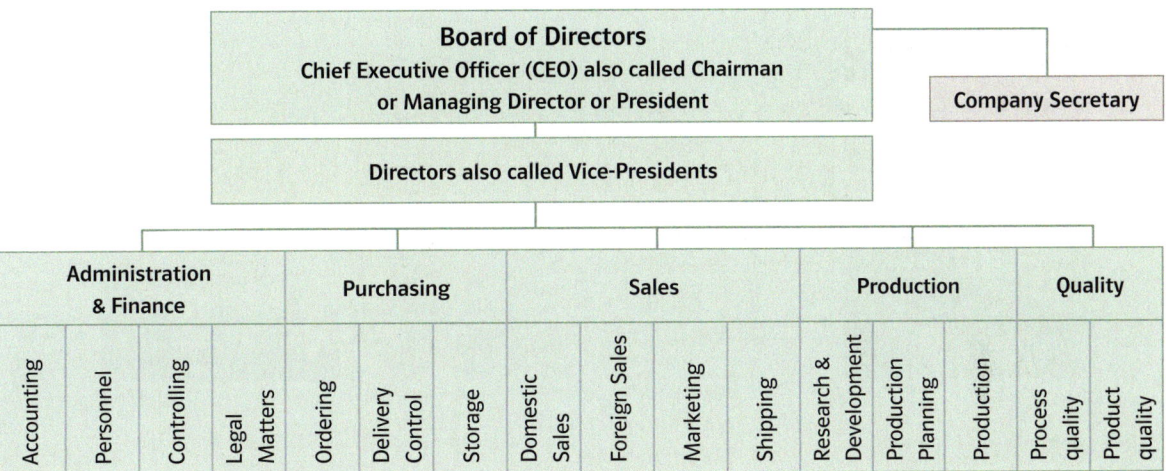

9 | Titles in British and US companies

Titles in British and US companies can be rather puzzling, with increasing globalisation only adding to the confusion. Some knowledge of the legal structure of companies is a help in finding the German equivalents. The following table shows a few generally accepted equivalents.

Aktiengesellschaft (AG)	Public Limited Company (Plc)	Stock Corporation (Inc. or Corp.)
Vorstandsvorsitzender	Chief Executive Officer (CEO), Chairman of the Board of Directors	Chief Executive Officer (CEO), President
Kaufmännischer Vorstand	Commercial Director	Senior Executive Vice-President Administration
Exportleiter	Export Manager, Head of the Export Department	Export Director
GmbH	**Private LImited Company (Ltd)**	**Closed Corporation**
Geschäftsführer	(Managing) Director	General Manager, Managing Director
Vorsitzender der Geschäftsführung	Chairman of the Board of Directors	Chief Executive Officer (CEO), President
Gesellschafter	Shareholder, Member	Stockholder

10 | Types of packaging

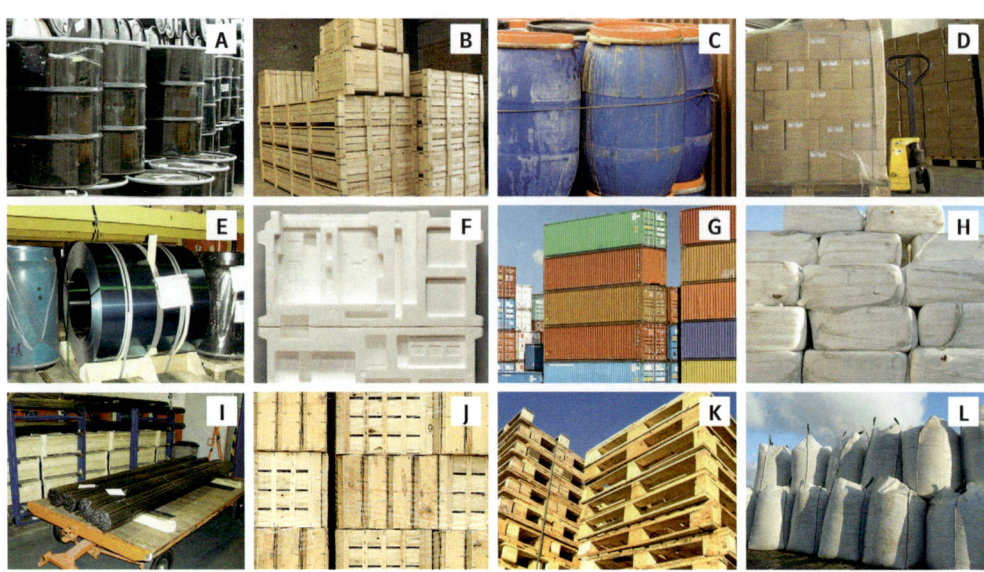

A	**drums** – Tonnen	**G**	**standard containers** – Standardcontainer
B	**wooden cases/boxes** – Holzkisten	**H**	**bales** – Ballen
C	**barrels** – Fässer	**I**	**bundles** – Bündel
D	**plastic foil** – Kunststofffolie	**J**	**crates** – Lattenkisten
E	**coil** – Coil, Rolle	**K**	**pallets** – Paletten
F	**polystyrene moulds** – Styroporform	**L**	**sacks** – Säcke

11 | Handling marks

A	fragile handle with care	**F**	radioactive
B	keep away from heat	**G**	top
C	centre of gravity	**H**	keep dry
D	use no hooks	**I**	flammable
E	sling here		

12 | Insurance

Exporters, importers and carriers take out insurance to protect themselves from risks of damage or loss of goods in transit. Insurance companies provide cover for such risks and compensate those insured
5 in the case of an incident.

Lloyd's of London is the "mother" of the insurance system and is an insurance market – not an insurance company, as many people think – where **underwriters**, either individuals or companies, and
10 syndicates form a pool to spread risk. Lloyd's, as it is generally called, goes back to Edward Lloyd, a coffee shop owner in London in the 17th century. His coffee shop in Tower Street and later in Lombard Street was a popular venue for sailors, merchants and ship
15 owners whom Lloyd provided with reliable shipping news. The deal-making that took place there led to the founding of the insurance market and of **Lloyd's Register**.

Since those days, the insurance business has come
20 a long way. Nowadays, marine/transport insurance is offered by many insurance companies worldwide. They provide **cover** against all manner of risks involved in the transport of goods against payment of a certain amount of money, called a **premium**
payable by the customer who wishes to insure the
25 goods to be transported or other risks in connection with transport. The calculation of the premium against which insurers offer cover is based on a variety of criteria such as which **Institute Cargo Clause** is chosen, value of the goods, nature of the
30 goods, transport route, means of transport, and risks insured. The insurance company's **underwriters** assess all these risks and calculate the premium accordingly.

The contract between a customer and an insurance
35 company is called a **policy**. All the details of the agreement between insurer and insured are laid down in this policy. Basically there are three different types of policy:

– **voyage policy**, which is taken out for one
40 individual shipment,
– **time or open policy**, which is taken out for a defined period of time, and
– **floating policy**, for which the insurance customer pays the premium as a lump sum in advance,
45 and which expires when this amount has been exhausted.

Under both the time policy and the floating policy **insurance certificates** are made out to accompany the consignment in question and to serve as ship-
50 ping/transport documents.

These basic policies have meanwhile been redesigned and adapted to modern transportation requirements. Thus, there are still **voyage policies, which serve as shipping documents** for individual
55 shipments, but companies which make regular shipments, will now take out **general** or **master policies**, which combine the characteristics of the former time and floating policies. These policies are always made out for one calendar year, i.e. from
60 01 January to 31 December of a given year and are subject to renewal. If such a policy is not concluded at the beginning of the year, it will be made out only until the end of that year.

Under **general** or **master policies** the insurer will
65 normally place blank, pre-signed certificate forms at the insured's disposal where they will be filled in with all the details relating to the shipment in question. These certificates serve as shipping documents, as the policy itself has obviously to remain with the
70 insured. Depending on what has been agreed in the insurance policy, customers have to inform their insurers of the number and details of all the certificates made out within a defined period, which can be on a monthly or quarterly basis. Failure to com-
75 ply with this obligation can lead to the insurer rejecting a claim. Renewal time is between September and end of year, when insurers and their customers negotiate the terms of the new contract.

There are **valued** and **unvalued** policies.
80 Under an **unvalued** policy the sum paid in the event of loss or damage is fixed according to the value of the goods at the time of the loss or damage.
Under a **valued** policy the amount of compensation to be paid in the event of loss or damage is fixed in
85 advance. Polices taken out for export shipments are valued policies. Insurance cover can be taken out for the total value of the goods plus 10% **imaginary profit**, to cover the profit the importer could have made, if the loss or damage had not occurred.

90 The scope of cover depends, among other things, on the **Institute Cargo Clauses** laid down by the Institute of London Underwriters. They are defined as Clauses A, B and C with Clause A covering all risks,

such as general average, particular average and damage from other causes. Some risks, however, among them war, nuclear risks, strikes, riots and civil commotion (SR & CC) are not even covered by an all-risks policy. Consequently, additional insurance has to be taken out to obtain compensation should these risks result in loss or damage.

Clauses B and C are more restrictive. **General average** is to be understood as deliberate loss, e.g. throwing cargo over board to save the ship. The loss has to be shouldered jointly by all owners of the cargo. **Particular average** refers to accidental loss and has to be borne by the owner of the goods in question.

Insurers provide cover for goods to be transported called **cargo insurance**. They offer cover for damage that may occur as a consequence of an incident or damage to the goods, which is called **consequential damage** or loss. They provide cover for transport incidents that involve people, which is called **third-party insurance**. And they offer cover for damage to a means of transport of their own insured or a third party, which is called **hull insurance**. For a few years carriers have been obliged to take out so-called **carrier's liability insurance** independently of any insurance that their customers may have for consignments to be transported. Carrier's liability has undergone a big overhaul and there is now much more responsibility on the carrier's part.

13 | Documents in foreign trade

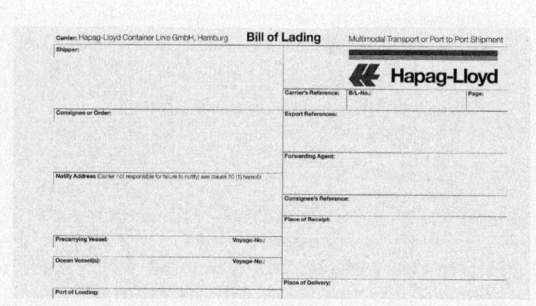

The **Bill of Lading** (B/L) (see page 202) is the most important document for transport by sea and for transportation involving at least two modes of transport, so-called multimodal transport. It is at the same time

– evidence of the contract of carriage between the shipper (exporter) and the carrier (shipping company)
– proof that the goods have been handed over to the carrier, i. e. a receipt for the goods
– a **document of title**. This means that anyone lawfully possessing the B/L is considered to be the rightful owner of the goods. Consequently, the ownership of the goods can be transferred by handing over the B/L, provided the B/L is made out "to order" (i. e. these two words appear in the box marked "consignee") and has been endorsed (signed on the back) by the person wishing to sell the goods. This makes it possible to sell goods while they are still at sea.

The B/L contains the names and addresses of the shipper and the consignee, a notify address if the B/L is made out to order, and details of the goods and the transport (description, weights, measurements, number of packages, marks, mode and route of transport, name of the vessel, port of shipment, port of destination, freight and other charges as well as the date of issue and reference numbers). It is usually completed and signed by the carrier, e. g. the captain of the ship, or by the carrier's agent. Should the carrier discover any defects or damage as regards the external condition of the packages he will make a note to this effect on the B/L. As a result the B/L will not be "**clean**" but "dirty", "foul" or "claused". The carrier may be preven-ted from clausing a B/L by a **letter of indemnity** from the shipper, whereby the shipper assumes any obligations resulting from the external defect of or damage to the packages.

Whenever a bank advances money for a trans-action under a letter of credit, it will insist on a clean, **on-board** B/L. On board means that the goods have actually been loaded on board ship. If no ship is available, the carrier issues a received-for-shipment B/L which can later be converted into an on-board B/L.

In case a B/L is marked 'surrendered' by a shipping agency, the exporter has paid all occurring costs for sea transport in advance. This B/L cannot be endorsed as ownership of the goods stays with the exporter. A copy of a surrendered B/L can be forwarded either by fax or e-mail. Ownership of the goods passes when the buyer settles the invoice including the stipulated sea fright costs for the consignment.

50 For multimodal transport, especially for container transport, the **FIATA Multimodal Transport Bill of Lading** (FBL) has replaced the combined transport B/L. FIATA is an interna-tional association of carri-ers.

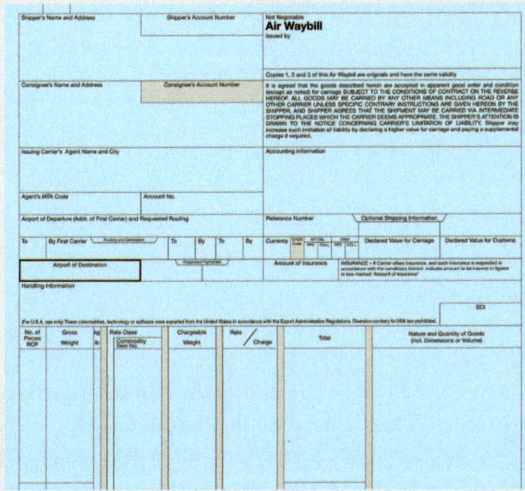

55 **Waybills**, also called consignment notes, are used in road, rail or air transport. They provide similar information to bills of lading and are likewise
– evidence of the contract of carriage
– and proof of the receipt of the goods but they do
60 not represent the goods as they are not docu-ments of title.

German exporters use the following waybills:
– for transport by rail the **CIM International Rail Consignment Note**
65 – for transport by road the **CMR International Consignment Note** (see page 203) and for EXW deliveries the **FIATA FCR (Forwarder's Certificate of Receipt)**
– for transport by air the **Air Waybill** (see
70 page 203)

Shipping documents are made out in aligned sets consisting of originals and copies for all parties involved. In the UK the Simple Trade Procedures Board (SITPRO Board) offers paper documents as
75 well as computer software to create them through its licensees.

Proforma Invoice (see Unit 9, page 149)

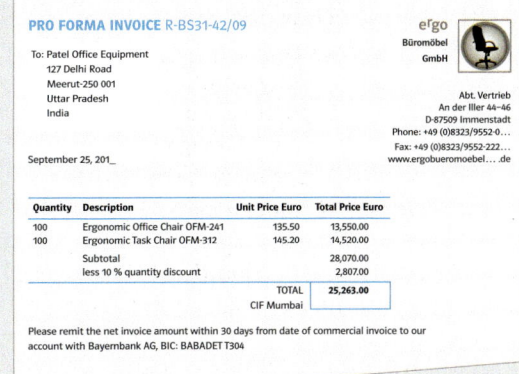

Commercial Invoice (see Unit 9, page 150)

Consular Invoice. This is an export invoice which
80 has been legalised by the consulate of the importing country. Such invoices are required by some Latin American countries for some goods as a true basis for charging import duty.

Customs Invoice. This is prepared and signed by the
85 exporter and a witness on an official form issued by the importing country and gives information as to the domestic value of the goods and the country of origin. It is required by Canada, Ghana, Israel, Nigeria and 9 other – smaller – states for customs
90 purposes.

Certificate of Origin (see page 204). This shows the country of origin of the goods or the country in which they were mainly produced. EU countries use a common form certifying that the goods are of
95 EU origin. Certificates of origin must be legalised, usually by a chamber of commerce. They may be required
– for political reasons (if, for instance, there are bans on imports from certain countries)
100 – if import quotas have been imposed on certain goods from certain countries
– if preferential duties have been agreed upon be-tween the exporting and importing countries.

Movement Certificate. This is a declaration made
105 by the exporter on the form EUR 1 and is attested by the customs authorities. It enables goods of EU origin to benefit from preferential rates of customs tariffs in 23 countries worldwide.

Export Declaration. Exports must be declared to the exporter's national customs authority on the appropriate forms (INTRASTAT) for statistical purposes.

Export Permit. This may be required by the exporting country if goods such as arms and weapons which are subject to export controls, are to be exported.

Test, Analysis, Weight Certificates and such like are issued by independent inspection authorities or by a certified producer. They provide some guarantee for the importer as to the quality and quantity of the goods.

Packing List. This is a detailed statement of the goods supplied in a particular consignment.

Insurance Policy/Certificate (see page 197).

14 | Organisations and associations

14.1 Organisations

United Nations (UN)
The UN was founded in 1945 to encourage peace and friendship among nations. Its stated aims are to facilitate cooperation between its 193 member states in international security, economic development, international law, social progress and human rights. The UN consists of several bodies, such as the General Assembly, the Security Council and the International Court of Justice and of a number of agencies, e. g. The World Health Organisation (WHO), the UN Children's Fund (UNICEF) and UNESCO, the UN Educational, Scientific and Cultural Organisation.

World Bank
The World Bank, founded in 1944 to finance post-war reconstruction, sees itself as a development institution owned by 188 member countries. It provides low-interest loans and grants to poor countries for education, health and infrastructure purposes.

International Monetary Fund (IMF)
The IMF, established in 1944, is an international organisation of 188 member countries. Its main responsibilities are promoting international monetary cooperation, facilitating international trade and granting credit to countries which are having difficulties re-paying or servicing debt.

World Trade Organisation (WTO)
The World Trade Organisation continues the work of Gatt (General Agreement on Tariffs and Trade), based on a treaty signed in 1947, with the aim of reducing or removing barriers to trade. Essentially the WTO is a negotiating forum for its 159 member countries. The agreements reached in lengthy negotiating rounds help trade to flow as freely as possible while allowing governments to meet social and environmental objectives.

Organisation for Economic Cooperation and Development (OECD)
The OECD comprises 34 wealthy countries committed to democracy and the market economy. Originally founded after the second world war to administer American aid to Europe, it is now one of the world's largest and most reliable sources of statistics and economic and social data. It provides a setting for governments to coordinate domestic and international policies.

14.2 Free trade areas and associations of states

The **European Economic Area (EEA)** embraces all the EU member countries plus Norway, Iceland and Liechtenstein. It provides for the free movement of people, goods (excluding agriculture and fisheries), services and capital between EEA countries. Swiss citizens have the right of abode in EEA countries although Switzerland is not a member of the EEA.

The **North American Free Trade Area (NAFTA)** came into being in 1994 and includes the United States of America, Canada and Mexico. The term "free trade area" implies that impediments to trade (particularly tariffs) have been phased out to facilitate the exchange of goods and services. Provisions regarding worker and environmental protection were added later to the trilateral agreement. Talks have begun to include other Latin American countries.

The **Association of Southeast Asian Nations (ASEAN)** was founded in 1967 and comprises Indonesia, Malaysia, The Philippines, Singapore, Thailand, Brunei, Laos, Myanmar and Cambodia. Its purpose is to accelerate economic growth, social progress and cultural development in the region and to promote regional peace and stability.

The **Mercado Común del Sur (MERCOSUR)** was founded in 1995 and comprises Argentina, Brazil, Paraguay, Uruguay and Venezuela, with Chile, Bolivia, Peru, Columbia and Mexico as associate members . Its purpose is to create a common market facilitating the free movement of goods and services, thus promoting economic and technological development.

The **Asia-Pacific Economic Cooperation (APEC)** is an inter-governmental grouping of 21 members established in 1989 to enhance economic growth and prosperity for the region around the Pacific rim by reducing tariffs and other trade barriers.

Asia-Pacific
Economic Cooperation

14.3 Economic Indicators

1. Balance of payments

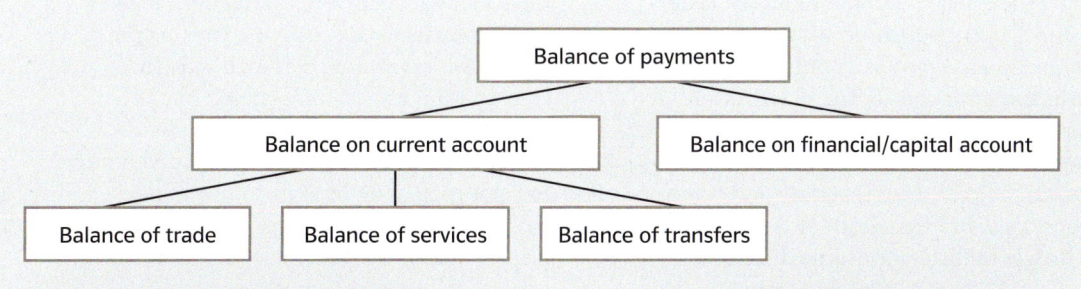

The **balance of payments** (Zahlungsbilanz) covers the total economic transactions of a country with the rest of the world during a specific period. It includes the following
5 balances.

The **balance on current account** (Leistungsbilanz) covers exports and imports of goods and services (without capital movements). It is made up of three balances.

10 1. The **balance of trade** (Handelsbilanz) covers trade in visible goods by value. If the value of goods exported is greater than that of imports the balance is in surplus. If the value of imports is greater than
15 that of exports the balance is in deficit. As Germany is one of the world's leading exporters of visible goods, its balance of trade has always been positive.

2. The **balance of invisible trade**
(Dienstleistungsbilanz) (also called balance
of services) is the balance of payments for
services rendered or received and includes
areas like transport, tourism, banking,
insurance, legal services, accountancy,
advertising and marketing, royalties, etc.
In Britain where this is the most dynamic
and rapidly growing sector of the economy
these products may be referred to as
"invisibles".

3. The **balance of transfers**
(Übertragungsbilanz) records a
country's contributions to international
organisations like the EU or the United
Nations, remittances by foreign workers
to their relatives in their home countries,
development aid and other transfers not
made in connection with trade.

The **balance on financial/capital** account
(Kapitalverkehrsbilanz) records inflows and
outflows of capital, e. g. for investment
purposes, viz. the net change in foreign
ownership of domestic assets.

15 | Distribution channels

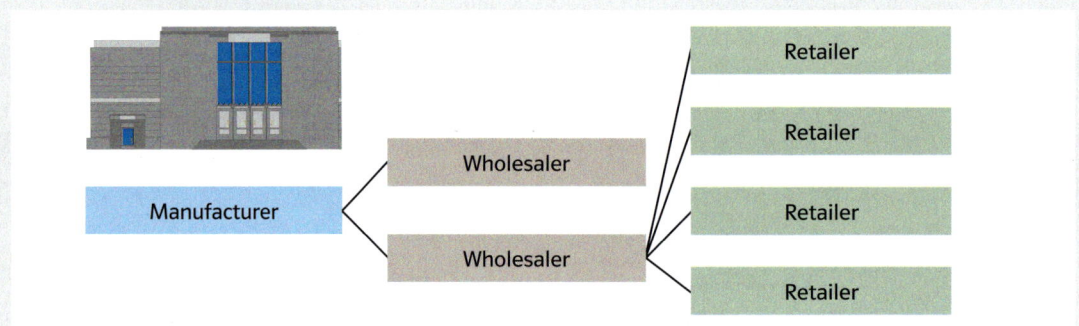

Traditional distribution channels have
undergone major changes in recent years
resulting from advanced communication
technologies and more sophisticated logistics.
Players at both ends of the distribution
chain, manufacturing industry and the retail
trade, have become more powerful in the
ongoing concentration and globalisation
process and are frequently in a position
to bypass traditional intermediaries by
direct purchasing or direct marketing. This
development has been facilitated by electronic
commerce, which is blurring the dividing
lines between retailers, wholesalers and mail-
order houses. This process of eliminating the
middleman, who represents a substantial cost
factor, is often called **disintermediation**.

Traditionally, **wholesalers** are the **links between manufacturers** and **retailers**. They
"break bulk", i. e. they buy large quantities
from the manufacturers, splitting them
up into smaller quantities, sometimes
repackaging them, and **distribute** these
smaller units to the retailers. For this purpose
they often maintain their own sales force and
fleet of vehicles. An important function of
wholesalers is **warehousing**, i. e. providing
suitable storage for goods, for example under
refrigeration. Wholesalers may also offer credit
facilities to their customers. The wholesale
trade is making use of the opportunities
offered by modern technology with its own
call centres and extranet links, enabling retail
customers to place orders 24 hours a day.
Advising customers on the nature and
application of products and services remains
one of the principal functions of wholesalers.

Retailers provide a local supply of goods
and offer a personal service to the general
public. They sell in small quantities and may
provide after-sales service where necessary.
There is a wide variety of different retail

outlets. The number of individual **specialist shops** has been falling over the years with

45 **chain stores** taking their place. Some chains specialise in a particular kind of merchandise, such as clothing, whereas the big grocery supermarkets offer some non-food items as well. **Department stores** sell an even wider

50 range of articles and try to provide a one-stop service for their customers. Generally, they are also operated by large chains. Other low-price retail chains offer a very basic service and range of goods to cut costs. Tradi-tional

55 **corner shops** have all but disappeared or have turned into 24 hour convenience stores. After a marked decline in numbers butchers, bakers, greengrocers and delicatessens seem to be making something of a comeback as

60 people demand better quality food. For small last-minute purchases kiosks, filling stations/ garages, and 24 hour stores provide a range of essential goods. "Armchair shopping" has a long tradition in the form of **mail-order**

65 **houses** which offer their goods via catalogues, the TV and the internet. Orders can be placed by post, telephone, e-mail or the internet. **E-commerce** is, however, not restricted to mail-order houses. Numerous businesses from travel

70 agents to banks and supermarkets have online operations or are purely online companies. It is an area of rapid growth but it is essential that logistics, i. e. the way the goods are delivered, are organised efficiently.

a

abbreviation Abkürzung

to abolish abschaffen

to accelerate beschleunigen

to access a file eine Datei aufrufen

access Zugang

accessories Accessoires, Zubehör

to accommodate Unterkunft bieten; entgegen-
kommen

accommodation Unterkunft

according to gemäß, in Übereinstimmung mit

accordingly folglich, demgemäß, dement-
sprechend

to account for ausmachen, entfallen auf

account holder Kontoinhaber(in)

account Konto, Benutzerkonto

accountability Haftung, Verantwortlichkeit

accountancy Wirtschaftsprüfung

accountant Rechnungs-, Wirtschaftsprüfer(in),
Buchhalter(in)

accounting Rechnungswesen

accounts department Buchhaltung, Rechnungswesen

accuracy Richtigkeit, Genauigkeit

to achieve erreichen, erzielen

to acknowledge bestätigen, anerkennen

to acquire erwerben

action Klage, Gerichtsverfahren

actual tatsächlich

additional fees zusätzliche Gebühren/Kosten

additional zusätzlich

to address anreden

adequate ausreichend

to adhere to (Vorschriften) einhalten

adjacent angrenzend, daneben

to adjoin angrenzen

to adjust anpassen, justieren, berichtigen

adjustment Anpassung, Beilegung(Beschwerde)

admin Verwaltung, Büroarbeit

to administer verwalten

administration and finance Verwaltung und
Finanzen

administrative body Verwaltungsbehörde

administrative charge Verwaltungsgebühr

administrative professions Verwaltungsberufe

to admire bewundern

to advance money Geld vorschießen

advanced fortgeschritten, fortschrittlich

advantageous vorteilhaft

adventurous risikobereit

advertising campaign Werbekampagne

advice of dispatch Versandanzeige

advisable ratsam, empfehlenswert

to advise benachrichtigen

advising bank avisierende Bank

to affect beeinflussen, beeinträchtigen,
betreffen

affiliated companies Konzerngesellschaften

affordable erschwinglich, bezahlbar

aforementioned oben genannt

after receipt of order nach Aufragseingang

after-sales service Kundendienst

age group Altersgruppe

agency agreement Vertretungsvertrag

agency Agentur, Unterorganisation

agreed upon vereinbart

air waybill Luftfrachtbrief

aisle Gang (z.B. im Flugzeug)

to alienate abstoßen, befremden

aligned aufeinander/zusammen passend

alleged angeblich, vermeintlich

to allocate zuweisen

allowance Zuschuss, Beihilfe

along national lines auf nationaler Basis

alongside neben

alteration Änderung

altogether ganz (und gar), gänzlich

to amend ergänzen, abändern, novellieren

amicable gütlich, freundlich

to amount to sich belaufen auf, betragen

And you! Ebenfalls!

annual general meeting Jahreshauptver-
sammlung

annual report Jahresabschlussbericht

annual jährlich

to antagonize ärgern, provozieren

apart from außer, abgesehen von

to apologise sich entschuldigen

apparent(ly) offensichtlich, anscheinend

to appeal to appellieren an, gefallen

appliance Gerät, Instrument

applicable zutreffend

applicant Bewerber(in)

application form Antragsformular

application Bewerbung, Anwendung

to apply to gelten für, betreffen, anwenden

to appoint ernennen

appreciation Wertschätzung, Würdigung,
Verständnis

apprentice Auszubildende(r)

apprenticeship Ausbildung

to approach sich annähern, sich wenden an,
ansprechen

approval Genehmigung, Billigung, Einver-
ständnis

to approve genehmigen, billigen

approximately etwa, ungefähr

arbitration Schlichtung, Schiedsgerichtsbarkeit

arbitrator Schlichter(in)

armchair shopping per Katalog oder online
einkaufen

arrears in payment Zahlungsrückstände

arresting ansprechend, ins Auge fallend

arrow Pfeil

artificial künstlich

as a whole insgesamt

as per gemäß, entsprechend

assembly hall Versammlungssaal

assembly Montage

to assess bewerten, einschätzen, abschätzen

asset Vermögenswerte

to assist helfen

assistance Hilfe

associate members assoziierte Mitglieder

to associate with in Verbindung bringen mit

association of carriers Spediteursvereinigung,
-verband

to assume liability Verantwortung übernehmen

to assume annehmen, übernehmen

assurance Zusicherung

to assure someone something jmdm. etwas
versichern

at a discount mit einem Abschlag/Rabatt

at fault schuldig

at most bestenfalls

at our expense auf unsere Kosten

at regular intervals in regelmäßigen Abständen

at short notice kurzfristig

at the latest spätestens

at the outset am Anfang

at your disposal zu Ihrer Verfügung

at your end bei Ihnen/Euch

at your risk and expense auf Ihre Verantwortung und zu Ihren Lasten

attachment Anhang (E-Mail)

(to) attempt versuchen; Versuch

to attend besuchen, teilnehmen

attention line Aufmerksamkeitszeile ("zu
Händen von")

to attest beglaubigen, bestätigen

to attract anziehen

authorised dealer Vertragshändler

to avoid vermeiden

to await warten

awareness Bewusstsein, Bekanntheitsgrad

awful scheußlich, schrecklich

a

back office Büro ohne Publikumsverkehr

back-up Unterstützung

to balance an account ein Konto ausgleichen,
saldieren

balance forwarded Saldoübertrag

balance of payments Zahlungsbilanz

balance Saldo

bale Ballen

ban on imports Einfuhrverbot

bank clerk Bankangestellte(r), Banker(in)

bank code Bankleitzahl

bank transfer Banküberweisung

banker's draft Bankscheck, Bankwechsel

banking industry Bankbranche

bar chart Balkendiagramm

bargaining position Verhandlungsposition

barriers to trade Handelshemmnisse

barter Tauschhandel

batch size Seriengröße

batch Produktionsmenge

to be in arrears in (Zahlungs)verzug sein

to be incorporated Körperschaftsstatus besitzen

to be into sth. etwas mögen, auf etwas stehen

to be lost in transit auf dem Transport verloren gehen

to be on sick leave krank geschrieben sein

to be on strike streiken

to be sued verklagt werden

to be on the lookout sich nach etwas umschauen, suchen

to be traded gehandelt werden

to be used to gewohnt sein

to bear in mind daran denken, nicht vergessen

to bear with s.o. etwas Geduld haben, so lange warten (am Telefon)

to bear tragen

bearer cheque Überbringer-, Inhaberscheck

beforehand im Voraus

beneficiary Begünstigte(r)

to benefit from Nutzen ziehen aus, profitieren

benefit (zusätzliche) Leistungen

beyond jenseits, außerhalb

bid Gebot, Kaufangebot

"big ticket" items teure Gebrauchsgüter

Bill of Exchange Act Wechselgesetz

bill of exchange Wechsel

bill of lading Konnossement

billboard Plakatwand

to blame die Schuld geben, verantwortlich machen

blank line Leerzeile

blank unbeschrieben, leer

blues Trübsinn

blunt unverblümt, geradeheraus

to blur verwischen

blurred verschwommen, unscharf

board of directors Unternehmensleitung, -vorstand

board Vorstand, Geschäftsleitung

body Behörde, Organisation

bold type Fettdruck

bond Anleihe, Obligation, Schuldverschreibung

bookkeeping Buchhaltung

to boost ankurbeln, fördern, verstärken

booth Messestand

to borrow entleihen, Kredit aufnehmen

to bother about sich kümmern um

bottom line Untergrenze , Fazit, Nettoprofit

branch office Filiale

brand Marke, Markenname

breach of contract Vertragsbruch

breach of treaty Vertragsbruch

to break bulk in großen Mengen einkaufen und in kleineren Mengen verkaufen

breakage Bruch

brief kurz

to brighten up aufhellen, aufheitern

to bring up the rear das Schlusslicht bilden

brochure Broschüre, Prospekt

broker (Börsen)makler(in)

brokerage Courtage, Maklerprovision

budget Haushalt

buffet lunch Mittagessen in Form eines Buffet

building contractors Bauunternehmen

bulk container Massengutcontainer

bulletin Newsletter, Mitteilungsblatt

bundle Bündel

buoyant lebhaft, florierend

business and corporate world Geschäfts- und Unternehmenswelt

business conduct Geschäftsgebaren

by conduct (Zustimmung) durch konkludentes Verhalten (durch ein Verhalten, das Zustimmung ausdrückt)

to bypass umgehen

C

to call for verdienen, verlangen

to call upon auffordern

to cancel absagen, stornieren, kündigen

cancellation Stornierung, Annullierung

capital goods Anlagegüter

capital letter Großbuchstabe

carbon copy Durchschlag mittels Kohlepapier

cardboard box Pappkarton

careless achtlos, unvorsichtig

carers Pflegepersonal, Betreuer

cargo capacity Ladekapazität

cargo liner Frachtschiff im Linienverkehr

caring fürsorglich

carriage forward unfrei, Fracht bezahlt Empfänger

carriage Transport, Transportkosten, Lieferung

carrier Frachtführer, Transportunternehmen

to carry a decision eine Entscheidung annehmen/verabschieden

case sensitive abhängig von Groß- und Kleinschreibung

cash discount Skonto, Barzahlungsrabatt

cash on delivery Zahlung per Nachnahme

cash with order Bezahlung bei Auftragserteilung

casual dress Freizeitkleidung

to cater for etwas bieten für

catering Verpflegung

caution marks Vorsichtsmarkierungen

cautious vorsichtig

celebration Feier

central heating installer Heizungsbauer(in), -installateur(in)

centre of gravity Schwerpunkt

certificate of analysis Analysebescheinigung

certificate of origin Ursprungszeugnis

certified producer zertifizierter Hersteller

certified beglaubigt

chain store Ladenkette

chairman of the board of directors Vorstandsvorsitzender

challenge Herausforderung

changeable wechselhaft

channels Wege, Kanäle

to charge with betreuen mit, verpflichten

charge Kosten, Gebühr, Belastung

to charge berechnen

charity wohltätige/gemeinnützige Organisation

chief accountant Leiter(in) des Rechnungswesens

chief engineer leitende(r) Ingenieur(in)

chilly kühl, frostig

chipped beschädigt, angeschlagen

circumstances Umstände

civil court procedures Zivilverfahren

claim for payment Zahlungsanspruch, -forderung

to claim Herausgabe verlangen

claim Behauptung

to clause a B/L Konnossement als unrein verzeichnen

clean rein(Konnossement)

to clear the balance den Saldo ausgleichen

to clear through customs verzollen

clerical staff Büropersonal, Sachbearbeiter

close business associate enger Geschäftsfreund

closely related eng verwandt

to codify kodifizieren

to collaborate zusammenarbeiten

collateral Sicherheiten, Pfand

to collect abholen, (ein)sammeln

collection agency Inkasso-Unternehmen

collection series Serienschreiben für das Inkasso

collocation Kollokation, Wendung

combed gekämmt

to come across wirken , zufällig finden

to come into being entstehen

to come into existence entstehen

to come up to entsprechen

to command verlangen, erwarten

commercial invoice Handelsrechnung

commercials Radio- und Fernsehwerbung, Werbespots

commission agent Handelsvertreter(in)

to commission in Auftrag geben

commission Provision

commissioner Kommissar(in)

to commit oneself sich festlegen, sich engagieren, sich verpflichten

commitment Verpflichtung

commodity Ware, Rohstoff

community Gemeinde, Gemeinschaft

comparable vergleichbar

comparatively vergleichsweise

to compensate entschädigen

competition Konkurrenz, Wettbewerb

competitor Mitbewerber(in), Wettbewerber(in)

to compile zusammenstellen, zusammentragen, -stellen

complaint Beschwerde, Reklamation

to complete ausfüllen (Formular)

complimentary close Grußformel am Schluss (Brief/Fax/E-Mail)

complimentary kostenlos, gratis

to comply with erfüllen, einhalten

components (Zubehör)teile, Komponenten

comprehensive umfassend

to comprise umfassen

to compromise Kompromiss eingehen, finden

compulsory liquidation Zwangsliquidation, -vergleich

computer projector Beamer

to concede einräumen, gewähren

conceited eingebildet

concerned besorgt

concession Zugeständnis, Konzession

conciliatory versöhnlich, konziliant

concise exakt, kurz und bündig

to conclude a contract einen Vertrag abschließen

to conclude abschließen

condemnation Verurteilung

condition Bedingung

to conduct durchführen

to confer übertragen, verleihen

conference chairs Konferenzraumbestuhlung

conference room Konferenzraum/-saal

confidence Vertrauen

confident überzeugt, zuversichtlich

confidential vertraulich

to confine oneself sich beschränken

to confirm bestätigen

congestion Verkehrsstau

connections Beziehungen

consent Zustimmung

consequences Folgen

consequential damage Folgeschaden

consequently daher, folglich

considerable beträchtlich

consideration Betrachtung, Erwägung, Gegenleistung

consignee Empfänger, Konsignatar

consignment note Frachtbrief

consignment Lieferung, Sendung

to consist of bestehen aus

to constitute darstellen, bilden

construction industry Bauindustrie

consular invoice Konsulatsfaktura

consumer Verbraucher(in)

to contain enthalten, beinhalten

containerisation Einsatz von Containern

content Inhalt

contract of carriage Beförderungsvertrag

contract Vertrag

to contract vertragliche Verpflichtung eingehen

to contribute beitragen

convenience store kundenfreundlicher Laden in der Nähe

convenient günstig gelegen, günstig

convention Versammlung, Tagung

conventional herkömmlich, konventionell

conversely umgekehrt, im Gegenzug

to convey vermitteln

conveyor belt Förder-, Montageband

to convince überzeugen

co-operative Kooperative, Genossenschaft; entgegenkommend

to cope with fertig werden mit

cordial herzlich

corporate customers Firmenkunden

corporate Firmen-

corporation Körperschaft

cost estimate Kostenvoranschlag

Council of Ministers Ministerrat

counterpart das Gegenüber, der Gegenpart, das Gegenstück

coupled with gekoppelt mit

court action Gerichtsverfahren, Klage

courtesy Höflichkeit

to cover decken

cracked gesprungen

craft Handwerk

crate Lattenkiste

to create legal relations ein Rechtsverhältnis eingehen

to create schaffen

creation Schaffung, Entstehen

credit agency Auskunftei

to credit an amount to an account einen Betrag einem Konto gutschreiben

credit facilities Kreditmöglichkeiten, Krediteinrichtungen

credit line Kreditlinie, -rahmen

credit note Gutschrift

credit period Zahlungsziel

credit standing Kreditwürdigkeit

to credit to an account einem Konto gutschreiben

credit Haben(seite)

creditor Gläubiger(in)

creditworthiness Kreditwürdigkeit

cross-border grenzüberschreitend

crossed cheque Verrechnungsscheck

crystal bowl Kristallschale

currency risk Währungsrisiko

current account Girokonto

current aktuell, gegenwärtig

currently zur Zeit, derzeit, gegenwärtig

curt schroff

customary gebräuchlich, üblich

custom-designed maßgeschneidert

customer service Kundendienst

customs authorities Zollbehörden

customs invoice Zollfaktura

customs tariff Zolltarif

customs Zoll

cutlery Besteck

(to be at the) cutting edge auf dem neuesten Stand sein

cyclamen Alpenveilchen

d

damage Beschädigung, Schaden

dash Gedankenstrich

database Datenbank

date of issue Ausstellungsdatum

daunting Respekt einflößend

deadline (letzte) Frist, Termin

to deal with behandeln, erledigen

to debit an account ein Konto belasten

debit card EC-Karte, Debitkarte

debit note Lastschriftanzeige

to debit belasten

debit Soll(seite)

debtor Schuldner(in)

decanter Karaffe, Dekanter

to decide beschließen

to decline zurückgehen, fallen, abnehmen

to deduct abziehen

to deem betrachten

to default on payment nicht bezahlen, eine Zahlung nicht leisten

defect Fehler, Mangel

definitely auf jeden Fall, eindeutig

to deflate die Luft herauslassen

to defray zahlen, decken, tragen (Kosten)

degree of security Sicherheitsgrad

degree Grad

del credere commission Delkredereprovision

to delay verzögern

delayed verzögert

to delete löschen

to deliver liefern

delivery deadline letzter Termin für die Lieferung

demand Bedarf, Nachfrage

to demonstrate zeigen, vorführen

dented verbeult

Department of Trade and Industry (GB) Ministerium für Handel (und Industrie)

to depend on abhängen von

depending on abhängig von, je nach

to deposit money Geld einzahlen

deposit Einlage

deputy (Stell)vertreter(in)

desk research Forschung am Schreibtisch

despite trotz

destined for bestimmt für

to destroy zerstören

to detail bestellen, mit einer Aufgabe betreuen

details Einzelheiten

to deteriorate schlechter werden, sich verschlechtern

determinable bestimmbar

diameter Durchmesser

diction Sprechweise

to differ from sich unterscheiden von

digit Ziffer

to diminish verringern

direct debiting Lastschrifteinzug

direct equivalent genaue Entsprechung

direction Leitung

dirty unrein(Konnossement)

to disappoint enttäuschen

discerning anspruchsvoll, kritisch

disconcertingly irritierenderweise

discreet diskret, zurückhaltend

discrepancies Unstimmigkeiten

discretion Ermessen

disintermediation Ausschaltung des Mittelsmanns

dismal trostlos

to dismantle abbauen, auseinandernehmen

(to) dispatch versenden; Versand, Absendung

to display zeigen, ausstellen

disposal Verfügung

to dispose of loswerden, veräußern, abstoßen

dispute Streitigkeiten

to disregard nicht beachten, als gegenstandslos ansehen

to disrupt stören

dissatisfied unzufrieden

distinct unterschiedlich

to distribute vertreiben, verteilen, ausschütten

distribution channel Vertriebsweg

distribution Vertrieb, Verkauf, Verteilung

distributor (Vertrags)händler(in)

dividend Dividende

dividing line Trennungslinie

division Sparte, Bereich

do (colloquial) Feier, Veranstaltung (umgangssprachlich)

to dock at anlegen an/in

document of title Eigentumsurkunde

documentary credit Dokumentenakkreditiv

documents against acceptance Dokumente gegen Akzept

documents against payment Dokumente gegen Bezahlung, Kassa gegen Dokumente

documents for collection Dokumenteninkasso

domestic value Inlandswert

domestic inländisch, heimisch

domiciled mit Sitz in (Land)

donation Spende

doubt Zweifel

down payment An-, Abschlagszahlung

downside Nachteil, Kehrseite

downturn Abschwung

(to) draft entwerfen; Tratte (Wechsel), Entwurf

to draw a bill on s.o. auf jmdn. einen Wechsel ziehen

to draw a cheque einen Scheck ziehen

to draw attention to Aufmerksamkeit lenken auf

drawback Haken, Nachteil

drawee Bezogene(r)

drawer Aussteller(in)

to drop sinken, fallen

due date Fälligkeitsdatum

due to wegen, aufgrund

due fällig

duration Dauer

e

ease Bequemlichkeit, Leichtigkeit

economical sparsam, wirtschaftlich

economy (Volks)wirtschaft

to effect durchführen, leisten

to elect wählen

to eliminate ausschalten

embarrassment Verlegenheit

embrace umfassen

to embroider on the truth die Wahrheit ausschmücken

to empathise sich einfühlen, sich hineinversetzen

to emphasise betonen

to employ einsetzen, verwenden

employee Beschäftigte(r), Angestellte(r)

employment Beschäftigung

en suite facilities Zimmer mit Bad und WC

to enable in die Lage versetzen

to enclose beifügen

enclosed beigefügt (Anlage beim Brief)

enclosure Anlage (Brief)

to encourage fördern, ermutigen

to endeavour sich bemühen

to endorse indossieren, im Amt bestätigt werden

endorsement Indossament

engaged besetzt (Telefon)

to enhance aufwerten, verstärken, erhöhen, verbessern

to enquire about sich erkundigen

enquiry Anfrage, Erkundigung, Untersuchung

ensuite bathroom eigenes Bad (Hotelzimmer)

to ensure dafür sorgen, sicherstellen, gewährleisten

to enter into an agreement eine Vereinbarung eingehen

to enter eingeben, ein-, betreten

to entertain unterhalten, sich kümmern um

entire ganz, vollständig

entitled berechtigt

entity Einheit, Rechtspersönlichkeit

to entrust with beauftragen mit, anvertrauen

entry Eintrag

enunciation Sprechweise

environment-friendly umweltfreundlich

equipped with ausgestattet mit

equity Eigenkapital, Aktien, Anteile

equivalent Entsprechung, Äquivalent

error Fehler, Versehen

essential sehr wichtig, wesentlich, notwendig, unbedingt erforderlich

to establish gründen, herausfinden

estate agent Immobilienmakler(in)

to esteem wertschätzen, achten

estimated delivery date voraussichtlicher Liefertermin

European Commission Europäische Kommission

European Court of Justice Europäischer Gerichtshof

European Parliament Europäisches Parlament

to evaluate bewerten, auswerten

even though obwohl, wenn auch

ever more important immer wichtiger

evidence Beweis(mittel), Nachweis, Beleg

ex stock ab Lager

exaggeration Übertreibung

to exceed übersteigen, übertreffen

excerpt Auszug

excess überschüssig

(to) exchange austauschen; Börse

to exclude ausschließen

exclusive right of sale Alleinverkaufsrecht

to execute durchführen, realisieren

executive board Vorstand

executive chair Chefsessel

executive functions Geschäftsführungs- aufgaben

executive suite Luxussuite

executive leitende(r)Angestellte(r), Führungskraft

executive Exekutive (= Regierung)

to exhibit zeigen, ausstellen

exhibitor Aussteller

exhibits Exponate, Ausstellungsgegenstände

exorbitant (maßlos) übertrieben, unverschämt

to expand erweitern, expandieren

to expedite beschleunigen

to expend ausgeben, verbrauchen

expenditure Auslagen

expense Kosten

experience Erfahrung(en)

expertise Kompetenz, Fachkenntnis

to expire ablaufen

expiry date Ablaufdatum, Verfallstermin

export clerk Exportkaufmann/-frau

export credit insurance Ausfuhrkredit- versicherung

export declaration Ausfuhrerklärung

export merchant Exporthändler(in)

export permit Ausfuhrgenehmigung

to expose to aussetzen

expressly ausdrücklich

to extend verlängern, erweitern, ausweiten

extension Nebenstelle, Durchwahl, Verlängerung, Aufschub

extent Ausmaß

extra zusätzlich

eye-catching auffallend, attraktiv

f

fabric sample Stoffmuster

face value Nennwert, eingetragener Wert

face Vorderseite

face-to-face persönlich

to facilitate ermöglichen, erleichtern

facilities Einrichtungen

factor Kommissionär(in)

factoring Factoring, Ankauf von Forderungen

to fail unterlassen

failing that wenn das nicht möglich ist

failure Unterlassung

fair Messe

fairly einigermaßen

Fairtrade products Produkte aus fairem Handel

faithful sinngetreu

fall-back position Rückzugsposition

faultless fehlerfrei

faulty workmanship Verarbeitungsfehler

favour Gefallen

favourable positiv, günstig

feature Eigenschaft, Merkmal

to feel obliged to sich verpflichtet fühlen

fees Gebühren

female addressee Adressatin

fidelity discount Treuerabatt

field research Feldforschung

fierce stark, heftig

to figure out herausfinden

figures Zahlen

to file a claim einen Anspruch anmelden

file Akte(nordner), Datei

to finalise zum Abschluss bringen

financial account Abrechnung, Rechnungs- legung

financial standing finanzieller Status

to find out feststellen

firm offer festes/verbindliches Angebot

firm fest

first thing als Erstes

fixed deposit account Festgeldkonto

flammable leicht entzündlich

flat flach, unverändert

fleet of vehicles Fahrzeugpark

flier Faltblatt

floating policy Abschreibepolice

for that matter (übrigens) auch, und auch

to fluctuate schwanken, sich ständig ändern

fluctuation Schwankung, Fluktuation

focus Schwerpunkt

folder Werbemappe

foothold fester Stand, sichere Stellung

to be on a familiar footing with sb vertraut sein mit jmdm.

for days on end tagelang

for instance zum Beispiel

for the account of auf Rechnung von

for the time being zunächst einmal, vorerst

Foreign Affairs auswärtige Angelegenheiten

foreign currencies ausländische Währungen, Devisen

foreign language correspon- dent Fremdsprachenkorrespondent(in)

foreign trade Außenhandel

fortune Glück, Vermögen

forward exchange dealings Devisentermingeschäfte

to forward absenden, weiterleiten

forwarder's certificate of receipt Spediteurüber- nahmebescheinigung

forwarding agent Spediteur

forward-looking zukunftsorientiert

fragile zerbrechlich

fragmented gespalten, zerstückelt

fragrant duftend

franchisee Franchisenehmer

franchising Franchisevergabe, Konzessions- verleihung

franchisor Franchisegeber

free movement of goods freier Warenverkehr

free movement Freizügigkeit

free of charge kostenfrei, umsonst

freight handling Beförderung von Fracht

freight prepaid Fracht bezahlt

freight Fracht

frequently häufig

from stock ab Lager

front office Büro mit Publikumsverkehr

fully liable voll haftbar

function room Veranstaltungsraum

to fund finanzieren

fundraising event Spendenveranstaltung

to furnish zur Verfügung stellen

furthest am weitesten

g

to gain a foothold Fuß fassen

gale force winds orkanartige Winde

gap Lücke

garment Kleidungsstück

to gather sammeln, entnehmen

general average allgemeine/große Havarie

to generate erzeugen

generous großzügig

germ Keim

to get down to business zur Sache/zum Geschäftlichen kommen

to get hold of erreichen

to get involved in sich engagieren in

ghastly entsetzlich

gist Kernaussage, das Wesentliche

to give due notice fristgerecht kündigen

to give notice kündigen

to give prominence to hervorheben

to give someone a message jmdm. etwas ausrichten

gloom Dunkelheit, Trübsinn

glucose-level meter Blutzuckermessgerät

to go bankrupt bankrott gehen

to go down well gut ankommen

to go for sich entscheiden für

to go wrong falsch laufen, schief gehen

go-ahead grünes Licht

goal Ziel

goodwill Wohlwollen, ideeller Firmenwert

to govern regeln

gradual allmählich, stufenweise, nach und nach

to grant credit Kredit gewähren

grant Beihilfe, Unterstützung

graphic representation grafische Darstellung

to grasp greifen, festhalten

grateful dankbar

greengrocer Gemüsehändler(in)

grid Gitter, Tabelle, Raster

groceries Lebensmittel

Gross Domestic Product Bruttoinlandsprodukt

gross brutto

ground floor Erdgeschoss

ground plan Grundriss

growth Wachstum

guarantee Garantie

h
_____

habit Gewohnheit, Angewohnheit

to hand over überreichen

handicrafts Kunstgewerbe, kunstgewerbliche Objekte

to handle handhaben, behandeln

handling fee Bearbeitungsgebühr

handling marks Behandlungsmarkierungen

handouts Handzettel

harmonisation Angleichung, Vereinheitlichung

haulage company Spedition

to have discounted diskontieren lassen

to have no option but keine andere Wahl haben, als …

head buyer Chefeinkäufer(in)

head of department Abteilungsleiter(in)

head of exports Leiter(in) der Exportabteilung

head of government Regierungschef(in)

head office Hauptverwaltung

headed geleitet

hearty herzhaft, deftig

heavy-duty hochleistungsfähig, strapazierfähig

hedging (Wechsel)kursabsicherung

heightened concern erhöhte Besorgnis

hence daher

hereinafter hiernach

herewith hiermit

hidden versteckt

High Representative Hohe(r) Vertreter(in)

high-end gehoben

higher commercial college Höhere Handelsschule

to hit treffen, negativen Einfluss haben

hitch Haken, Problem

to hold liable haftbar machen

to hold responsible verantwortlich machen

holder Inhaber(in)

holding company Holding, Mutter-, Dachgesellschaft

to honour honorieren, einlösen

hook Haken

hospitality Bewirtung von Gästen, Gastfreundschaft

host country Gastland

to host Gastgeber sein

hostile feindlich

hot rolled stainless steel warm gewalzter Edelstahl

How are you getting on? Wie geht es Ihnen/Dir?

hug Umarmung

huge riesig

hull insurance Kaskoversicherung

hurdle Hürde, Hindernis

hyphen Bindestrich

i
_____

if applicable falls zutreffend

ill-considered unüberlegt

illustrated brochure Broschüre mit Bildern

I'm afraid leider

imaginary profit angenommener Gewinn

to imagine sich vorstellen

immediately unverzüglich, sofort

impact Wirkung, Einfluss

to impair beeinträchtigen

impediments Hindernisse, Hemmnisse

impending kurz bevorstehend

imperative dringend erforderlich

imperfections Unvollkommenheiten

to implement umsetzen

to imply beinhalten, bedeuten

impolite unhöflich

import duty Einfuhrzoll

import quota mengenmäßige Einfuhrbeschränkung, -kontingent

to impose a fine eine Geldstrafe/-buße verhängen

to impose verhängen, auferlegen

impressive beeindruckend

in advance im Voraus

in arrears in Verzug

to be in charge of verantwortlich sein für

in charge zuständig

in connection with im Zusammenhang mit

in due time termingerecht

in exchange for im Austausch gegen

in favour of zugunsten

in full in voller Höhe, vollständig

in good time rechtzeitig

in haste übereilt, hastig

in keeping with in Einklang mit

in line with in Übereinstimmung mit, parallel zu

in one's own right aus eigenem Recht

in our favour zu unseren Gunsten

in possession of im Besitz

in quadruplicate in vierfacher Ausfertigung

in recent months in den letzten Monaten

in rotation nach dem Rotationsprinzip

in that da

in the course of im Laufe von

in triplicate in dreifacher Ausfertigung

in view of angesichts

in working order funktionsfähig

in writing schriftlich

inability Unfähigkeit

inadequate unzulänglich

incident Vorfall

inclination Neigung

inconvenience Unannehmlichkeit

to incorporate einbeziehen, einarbeiten

to incur debts Verbindlichkeiten eingehen, Schulden machen

to incur losses Verluste erleiden

to indemnify entschädigen

in-depth in die Tiefe gehend

to indicate angeben, zeigen

indifferent gleichgültig

indispensable unverzichtbar

industry Branche

inflation rate Inflations-, Teuerungsrate

ingredients Zutaten

inherent innewohnend, zugehörig

to inherit erben

initial order Erstauftrag

initial anfänglich

initials Anfangsbuchstaben, Initialen

to initiate einleiten, anbahnen, initiieren

inland waterway vessel Binnenschiff

to insert einfügen, einschieben

to insist on bestehen auf

insistent bestimmt (Ton), drängend, nach-
drücklich

insolvent zahlungsunfähig

inspection authority Prüfstelle

inspection certificate Prüfbescheinigung

instalment Rate

instant access sofortiger Zugriff

to institute legal proceedings gerichtlich
vorgehen, Klage erheben

to instruct anweisen, beauftragen

instruction Anweisungen

to insulate isolieren

insurance packages Versicherungspakete

insurance policy Versicherungspolice

insurance Versicherung

interest on arrears Verzugszinsen

interface Schnittstelle

interference Interferenz, Störung

interior decorating firm Inneneinrichtungs-
unternehmen

interior designer Innenarchitekt(in)

intermediary Zwischenhändler, Mittelsmann

to intermingle (sich) vermischen

internship Praktikum

to interpret dolmetschen

intertwined verflochten, miteinander verknüpft

interviewee Befragte(r)

intra-Community delivery innergemeinschaft-
liche Lieferung

introductory discount Einführungsrabatt

intrusive aufdringlich

invaluable unschätzbar, unbezahlbar

invasive aufdringlich

to investigate erforschen, untersuchen,
recherchieren

investigative erforschend

investment fund Investmentfonds

invisibles Dienstleistungen

invitation Einladung

invoice amount Rechnungsbetrag

invoice Rechnung

to invoice in Rechnung stellen

to involve beinhalten

to iron out lösen, glätten

irregular unregelmäßig

irrespective of unabhängig von

irrevocable letter of credit unwiderrufliches
Akkreditiv

irrevocable unwiderruflich

to issue a receipt eine Quittung ausstellen

issue Frage, Thema, Problem, Ausgabe (einer
Zeitung)

to issue ausstellen, ausgeben

it goes without saying es ist selbstverständlich

items Posten

itinerary Reiseroute

j

job description Stellenbeschreibung

job interview Vorstellungsgespräch

joint stock company Kapitalgesellschaft

joint venture Joint Venture

jointly gemeinsam

judge Richter(in)

to juggle jonglieren, hin und herschieben

to jumble durcheinander werfen/bringen

junior Nachwuchs-

justified gerechtfertigt

jute Jute

k

keen bestrebt, sehr daran interessiert

to keep an account Buch führen, festhalten,
niederschreiben

to keep the minutes Protokoll führen

to keep up with sth. mit etwas mithalten

key interest rates Leitzinsen

kitchenette Teeküche, Pantryküche

knitting Stricken

know it all Besserwisser

l

labour Arbeitskräfte

lack of Mangel an

landlady Vermieterin

landline/fixed line Festnetzanschluss

large-scale im großen Maßstab, groß angelegt

latter letztere/r/s

law Gesetz, Recht

lead Führung

league Liga

to learn erfahren

lease Miete, Pacht(verhältnis)

legal consequences juristische Folgen

legal entity juristische Person

legal pattern juristische Konstruktion

legal system Rechtssystem

to legalise beglaubigen

legislation Gesetze, Gesetzgebung

Leipzig-based mit Sitz in Leipzig

to lend ausleihen, Kredit gewähren

lengthy langwierig, lang

to let someone know jmdm. Bescheid geben

to let vermieten

letter of credit Akkreditiv

letter of indemnity Konnossementsgarantie

letterhead Briefkopf

liability Haftung

libel Verleumdung

licensee Lizenznehmer

licensing Lizenzvergabe

life cycle Lebenszyklus

likely wahrscheinlich

likewise gleichermaßen

limited liability beschränkte Haftung

limited partnership in etwa vergleichbar
einer KG

limited begrenzt

limp schlaff

line graph Liniendiagramm

line Branche

link Verbindung, Binde-, Kettenglied

linking word Binde-,Verbindungswort

liquid Flüssigkeit

literally buchstäblich, geradezu

litigation Rechtsweg, Rechtsprechung

loading charges Verladegebühr

loan Darlehen, Kredit

local authority Kommune, Stadtverwaltung

to locate ausfindig machen, orten

location Lage, Standort

to look up nachschlagen

loss Verlust, Schaden

low-interest loans Niedrigzinsdarlehen

lump sum Pauschale, Einmalzahlung

m

mail-order house Versandhaus

mailshots Postwurfsendungen

to maintain aufrechterhalten, warten,
unterhalten

maintenance and repair Wartung und Instand-
haltung

maintenance work Wartungsarbeiten

major bank Großbank

major bedeutend, größer, wichtig

to make out to order an Order ausstellen

to make up for wiedergutmachen

to make up erfinden

managing director Geschäftsführer(in)

manner Auftreten, Verhalten

to manufacture herstellen, anfertigen

marine insurance Seetransportversicherung

marine See-

marital status Familienstand, Personenstand

maritime insurance Seetransportversicherung

marked deutlich

market share Marktanteil

to market vermarkten

marking Markierungen

mass-market product Massenartikel

to materialise entstehen, eintreffen, Wirklich-
keit werden

maturity Fälligkeit (Wechsel), Reife

means of payment Zahlungsmittel

measurement instrument Messinstrument

to meet a commitment einer Verpflichtung
nachkommen

to meet a deadline eine Frist/einen Termin
einhalten

to meet an obligation einer Verpflichtung
nachkommen

to meet requirements Wünschen/Anforde-
rungen entsprechen

to meet up with someone sich mit jemandem
treffen

to mention erwähnen

merchandise Ware

merchants Kaufleute

merger Fusion

messaging Nachrichtenübermittlung

middle-income mittleres Einkommen

mill Fabrik, Hütte, Mühle

minimum share capital Mindestkapital

miscellaneous products sonstige Produkte

misleading irreführend

misunderstanding Missverständnis

to mix up with verwechseln

mix-up Verwechslung

to modify leicht ändern

moisture Feuchtigkeit

monetary währungs-, geld-, finanzpolitisch

to monitor beobachten, prüfen, kontrollieren

monochrome schwarzweiß, einfarbig

Monotype Corsiva Name einer Schriftart

more often than not meistens

moreover außerdem, überdies

mortgage Hypothek

motorway Autobahn

to move umziehen

movement certificate Warenverkehrs-
bescheinigung

multimodal mehrere Verkehrsmittel umfassend

mutual gegenseitig, beiderseitig

n

neatly ordentlich, säuberlich, übersichtlich

a note to this effect ein diesbezüglicher
Vermerk

necessarily notwendigerweise

to negotiate aus-, verhandeln

net netto

NGO Nichtregierungsorganisation

nominal share capital nominelles Eigenkapital

to nominate nominieren

non-attendance Abwesenheit

non-judgmentally unvoreingenommen

no-nonsense unverblümt, direkt

non-performance Nicht-Erfüllung

non-taxable nicht steuerpflichtig

to note down notieren, aufschreiben

noticeable auffällig, erkennbar, deutlich

notification Benachrichtigung

notify address Meldeadresse

to notify benachrichtigen

nursery Pflanzenschule, Gärtnerei, Kinder-
garten, Vorschule

nursing home Altersheim, Pflegeheim

o

obligation Verpflichtung

obligations Verbindlichkeiten

obliged verbunden, dankbar

to obtain erlangen, erhalten

to obviate umgehen, unnötig machen

obvious(ly) offensichtlich

occasion Anlass

to occur vorkommen

occurrence Vorkommnis, Vorfall

offeree Angebotsempfänger(in)

offeror Angebotssteller(in), Anbieter(in)

office management assistant etwa: Kaufmann/
-frau für Büromanagement, Bürokaufmann/
-frau

to offset ausgleichen

omission Auslassung

to omit aus-,weglassen

on a consignment basis in Kommission

on a modest scale in einem bescheidenen
Rahmen

on behalf of im Auftrag/Namen von, für

on delivery bei Lieferung

on demand auf Verlangen

on good authority aus glaubwürdiger Quelle

on hand zugegen, zur Verfügung, parat

on our part unsererseits

on receipt nach Erhalt

on request auf Anfrage

on site vor Ort

on the off-chance auf gut Glück, auf Verdacht

on-board B/L Bordkonnossement

one-off einmalig

one-side von einer Seite zugänglich

one-storey einstöckig

ongoing in Gang befindlich, laufend

on-site vor Ort

open account terms offenes Zahlungsziel,
Lieferantenkredit

open credit Zahlung gegen einfache Rechnung

open day Tag der offenen Tür

open policy Generalpolice

opening bank eröffnende Bank

opening freie Stelle

to operate tätig sein

operating manual Betriebsanleitung

opponent Gegner(in)

opposite number Gegenüber

to opt for sich entscheiden für

options Alternativen

order for payment Zahlungsbefehl

order on call Abrufauftrag

ordinary partnership in etwa vergleichbar einer
OHG

organic produce Bioprodukte

origin Ursprung

to originate entstehen, Ursprung haben,
zustande kommen

out of court außergerichtlich

outcome Ausgang, Ergebnis

outing Ausflug

outlet Verkaufsstelle

outstanding balance offener Saldo

outstanding ausstehend

overall insgesamt, übergreifend

overbearing überheblich

overcast bedeckt

overdraft credit Überziehungs-, Dispokredit

overdue überfällig

to overlook übersehen

overseas customers Kunden aus dem Ausland

overseas im Ausland

oversight Versehen

to owe schulden

ownership Eigentum(srecht)

p

PA Assistent(in), Sekretär(in)

Pacific rim Anrainerländer am Pazifik

package Packstück, Kollo (Plural Kolli)

packaging Verpackung

packing list Packliste

padding Polstermaterial

paragraph Absatz

to paraphrase umschreiben
parent company Muttergesellschaft
parking facilities Parkmöglichkeit
part payment Teilzahlung
participants Beteiligte, Teilnehmer
participation Teilnahme, Beteiligung
particular average einfache Havarie, Teilhavarie
particulars Einzelheiten
parties to the contract Vertragsparteien
partitioned aufgeteilt, unterteilt
partnership Personengesellschaft, Teilhaberschaft
to pass on weiterleiten, verabschieden
past due überfällig
pastures new neue Ufer (sich aufmachen zu neuen Ufern)
path Pfad, Weg
to pay attention to darauf achten
payee Zahlungsempfänger
payment in advance Vorauszahlung
payment on receipt of invoice Zahlung bei Rechnungserhalt
payment record (bisherige) Zahlungsmoral
peak Gipfel, höchster Punkt, Höhepunkt, Spitze
pending bis zum Eintreffen, in Erwartung
to perceive wahrnehmen
percentage Prozentsatz
perception Wahrnehmung
to perform durchführen
performance Erbringung, Leistung, Erfolg
periodical Zeitschrift
permission Erlaubnis
(to) permit erlauben; Erlaubnis, Genehmigung
persistent hartnäckig
to persuade überzeugen, überreden
persuasion Überzeugung, Überredung
persuasive überzeugend
to phase in schrittweise einführen
to phase out allmählich abschaffen, auslaufen lassen
to pick up sich erholen
to pick auswählen
pie chart Tortendiagramm
pillar Säule
to place an order einen Auftrag erteilen, eine Bestellung aufgeben
place of destination Bestimmungsort
placement Praktikum
to plough through sich hindurchquälen
plug Stecker
plumber Klempner(in)
to point out darauf hinweisen
to polish putzen, polieren
polythene bags Polyäthylenbeutel

poor appearance mangelhafte Erscheinung
poor grades schlechte Noten
port of shipment Verschiffungshafen
portfolio Aufgabenbereich
positioning Positionierung
postcode Postleitzahl
poster Plakat
to postpone auf-, verschieben
powers Befugnisse
practical Praktikum
precarious prekär, gefährdet, unsicher, bedenklich
precaution Vorsichtsmaßnahme
to precede vorangehen, -stehen, -stellen
precise präzise, genau
predecessor Vorgänger(modell)
predicament schwierige Lage, Dilemma, Zwangslage
preferably vorzugsweise
preferential duties Vorzugszölle
preliminary erste, vorläufige
premises Geschäftsräume, Firmengelände
pre-requisite Vorbedingung
Presidency Präsidentschaft
press release Pressemitteilung
pressure Druck
prestigious renommiert, angesehen
to presume annehmen
prevalence Vorkommen
previously vorher
principal Prinzipal, Auftraggeber
prior to vor, im Vorfeld von
priority Vorrang
private limited company in etwa vergleichbar einer GmbH
procedure Verfahren, Ablauf
proceedings Ablauf, Vorgehensweise
proceeds Erlöse, Einnahmen
to process be-, verarbeiten
to procure beschaffen, besorgen
to produce up to ISO DIN plus standards nach europäischen ISO DIN plus Standards produzieren
produce (landwirtschaftliche) Erzeugnisse
product liability insurance Produkthaftpflichtversicherung
profession Beruf
profit margin Gewinnspanne
profitable gewinnbringend, rentabel
profoundly tief, hochgradig
progress Fortschritt
to project an image einen Eindruck vermitteln
to prolong verlängern
prolongation Verlängerung

to promote fördern
prompt Hinweis, Stichwort
to pronounce on entscheiden, urteilen über
proof Beweis
to proofread Korrektur lesen
proper names Eigennamen
property insurance Gebäudeversicherung
property Immobilie, Eigentum
proposal Vorschlag
proprietor Inhaber(in)
prosperity Wohlstand
proven bewiesen
to provide zur Verfügung stellen, vorsehen
provision of services Erbringung von Dienstleistungen
provisions Vorschriften, Regelungen
public limited company in etwa vergleichbar einer AG
publication of accounts Veröffentlichung des Jahresabschlusses
publicly öffentlich
to pull the wool over someone's eyes jmdn. hinters Licht führen
punctual pünktlich
punctuation Interpunktion
purchase order Auftragsformular
to purchase kaufen
purchaser Käufer(in)
purchasing Einkauf
pure rein, ausschließlich
to put through durchstellen, verbinden

q

qualification berufliche Eignung, Fähigkeit
quantity discount Mengenrabatt
quarterly vierteljährlich
quay Kai, Dock, Anlegestelle
query Frage, Anfrage
questionnaire Fragebogen
quotation Preisangebot, Angebot, Kostenvoranschlag
to quote (Preis) angeben

r

rail consignment note Bahnfrachtbrief
to raise capital Kapital beschaffen
to raise (Thema) anschneiden, erhöhen
to rally sich versammeln, sich erholen
range of products Produktpalette, Sortiment
range Bereich, Auswahl, Sortiment
rash voreilig
rate of interest Zinssatz
rate Preis, Tarif
re bezüglich, betreffend

to read back wiederholen

Reading Council Stadtverwaltung/Stadtrat von Reading

readily available leicht erhältlich

ready market aufnahmebereiter Markt, Markt mit großer Nachfrage

real estate Immobilien

real-time information Auskunft über den aktuellen Stand

reasonable einigermaßen gut

rebate Nachlass, Rückvergütung

to recall zurückrufen

receipt Empfangsbestätigung, Quittung

received-for-shipment B/L Übernahmekonnossement

reception Empfang

recipient Empfänger(in)

to reciprocate sich revanchieren

to recommend empfehlen

to reconsider überdenken

reconstruction Wiederaufbau

to record aufzeichnen, aufnehmen

record Aufzeichnung, Unterlage, Dokument, Akte

records Unterlagen

to recruit einstellen

recruiter Einstellungssachbearbeiter(in)

to rectify richtig stellen, (Problem) beheben, berichtigen

redecoration Renovierung

to refer to sich beziehen auf, Rücksprache nehmen, weiterleiten, einreichen

referee empfehlende Person

reference number Kennziffer

reference Bezug(szeichen)

refill cartridge Ersatzpatrone, Nachfüllpatrone

refinement Verfeinerung

to reflect widerspiegeln

refund Erstattung

to refuse ablehnen, sich weigern

regardless of ungeachtet, unabhängig von

to register sich anmelden

Registrar of Companies in etwa: Handelsregister

to regret bedauern

regrettable bedauerlich

regulations Direktiven, Vorschriften

to rehearse proben

to reimburse erstatten

to reject ablehnen

to relate to in Kontakt kommen mit

to relax entspannen, lockern

to release freigeben, entlassen, befreien

relevant sachdienlich

reliable sources zuverlässige Quellen

to relocate umziehen

reluctance Abneigung, Widerwillen

to rely on sich verlassen auf

remainder Rest

remarks Bemerkung

remedy Abhilfe, Heilmittel, Lösung

reminder Mahnung, Erinnerung(schreiben)

to remit überweisen

remittance form Überweisungsträger

remote abgelegen

removable auswechselbar, herausnehmbar

remuneration Entgelt

to render impossible unmöglich machen

to render leisten

(to) rent mieten; Miete

to repackage umpacken

to re-pay zurückzahlen

repeat order Nachbestellung

repeatedly wiederholt, ständig

to replace ersetzen, austauschen

to report back sich zurückmelden

representation Vertretung

reputation Ruf

request Bitte, Anfrage

to require benötigen

requirement Anforderung

research and development Forschung und Entwicklung

reservation Vorbehalt

to reserve the right sich das Recht vorbehalten

resource (finanzielle) Mittel, Ressourcen

respectable angesehen

respective jeweilig

respectively bzw.

respite Atempause, Zahlungsaufschub

response Reaktion

to restrict einschränken, beschränken

retail chain Einzelhandelskette

retail outlet Einzelhandelsgeschäft

retailer Einzelhändler

to retain the profits den Gewinn einbehalten

to retain behalten

to return a favour sich revanchieren

to reveal offen legen, enthüllen

to reverse umdrehen

to revert zurückkehren, wieder annehmen

to revoke widerrufen

right away sofort, direkt

right of abode Wohnrecht

rigidity Starrheit

rigorous peinlich genau, gründlich

rival products Produkte der Konkurrenz

road haulage industry Straßenverkehrsbranche

ro-ro ferry Ro-Ro-Fähre (roll on roll off)

rough handling unsachgemäße Behandlung

roughly ungefähr, in etwa

round Runde

royalties Tantiemen, Lizenzgebühren

royalty Nutzungsgebühr, Tantieme

ruling (höchst)richterliche Entscheidung

to run an office ein Büro leiten

run up Vorbereitung, Vorlauf

to rush übereilt handeln

S

to safeguard sicher aufbewahren

safely sicher, ohne Gefahr

sale Verkäufe, Absatz

sales contract Kaufvertrag

sales literature Verkaufsunterlagen

salutation Begrüßung, Anrede(im Brief/E-Mail)

sample Stichprobe, Muster, Auswahl

satisfaction Zufriedenheit

satisfactory zufriedenstellend

savings account Sparkonto

to schedule zeitlich anberaumen

scope Umfang, Reichweite, Spielraum

scratched verkratzt

screen Bildschirm, Leinwand

search engine Suchmaschine

sector of industry Branche

securities Wertpapiere, Effekten

security Sicherheit

to see to dafür sorgen

to see your way clear to do sth. zustimmen, etwas zu tun

to seek to versuchen

self-catering flat Apartment mit Selbstverpflegung

self-financing selbstfinanzierend

senior executive leitende(r) Angestellte(r), Führungskraft

sensitive empfindlich

to separate (ab)trennen

service engineer Kundendiensttechniker(in)

to set about sich anschicken

to set up as sich selbständig machen als

to set up errichten, einrichten

to settle an account ein Konto ausgleichen, Verbindlichkeiten begleichen

to settle beilegen, erledigen, festlegen, abmachen, abrechnen

settlement Begleichung, (Be)zahlung, Regulierung

shareholder Aktionär(in), Anteilseigner(in)

shares Aktien, Anteile

shipment Lieferung

shipper Versender

shipping agent (Seehafen)spediteur

shipping company Reederei

shipping line Schifffahrtslinie, Reederei

ship's rail Schiffsreling

shortage Knappheit, Mangel

to shortlist eine erste Auswahl treffen

to shrink schrumpfen

shuttle service Pendelverkehr, Zubringerservice

sight draft Sichttratte

signatory Unterzeichner(in)

signature footer Unterschriftsfußzeile

signature Unterschrift

significant bedeutend

to simplify vereinfachen

sincerity Aufrichtigkeit

Single Market Binnenmarkt

size Größe(nordnung)

skilful geschickt

slash Schrägstrich

to sleep Schlafmöglichkeit bieten

slight gering

slip of paper Zettel

slowdown Verlangsamung, Abschwung

sluggish träge, stagnierend, flau, schleppend

smoothly reibungslos

sociable gesellig, kontaktfreudig

soiled beschmutzt

sole agency Alleinvertretung

sole proprietor Alleininhaber(in)

sole trader Einzelkaufmann, -frau

solicited verlangt

solicitor Rechtsanwalt, Rechtsanwältin

solution Lösung

solvency Solvenz, Zahlungsfähigkeit

solvent zahlungsfähig

to some extent bis zu einem gewissen Grad

sophisticated hochentwickelt

sorely missed schmerzlich vermisst

to sort sth. out etwas regeln, in Ordnung
bringen

sound knowledge gute, fundierte Kenntnisse

sound solide, gesund

to source sth. (from) etwas beziehen (von)

source Quelle

space Fläche

spacing Abstände

spare parts Ersatzteile

sparingly sparsam

sparkling mit Kohlensäure

specialist shop Fachgeschäft

specified einzeln angegeben

to specify genau bezeichnen

to speed up beschleunigen

speedy schnell

spend Budget, Ausgaben

to split up aufteilen

sports equipment Sportartikel, -ausrüstung

sportswear Sportbekleidung

spread Verbreitung

to spread verteilen

to squash quetschen, zerquetschen

to squirm sich winden

staff Mitarbeiter, Personal

to stage a comeback ein Comeback inszenieren

stage Bühne, Stadium

staggered payment gestaffelte Zahlung

staggered prices gestaffelte Preise

stained befleckt

to stamp stempeln

to stand out from sich abheben von

to stand to lose (höchst)wahrscheinlich
verlieren

standardised genormt

standing order Dauerauftrag

starting salary Anfangsgehalt

start-up neugegründete Firma

state of affairs Stand der Dinge

statement of account Kontoauszug

state-of-the-art auf dem neuesten Stand (der
Technik)

statute Parlaments-Gesetz

steady decline stetiger Rückgang

to stipulate vertraglich vereinbaren, festsetzen

stipulations Vertragsvereinbarungen, -bedin-
gungen

stock exchange (Wertpapier)börse

stock market analysts Börsenanalysten

stockholder Aktionär(in)

stocks Aktien

storage Lagerhaltung

to store (ein)lagern, speichern

straight away sofort, unverzüglich

to strengthen verstärken

strengths and weaknesses Stärken und
Schwächen

to stress betonen

stretch Strecke, Gebiet

stunning atemberaubend, umwerfend

sturdy wooden crate stabile Lattenkiste

sturdy stabil

styrofoam-padded mit Styropor ausgeschäumt

subconscious unbewusst

subject line Betreffzeile

subject matter Gegenstand, Thema

subject to change Veränderungen unterworfen,
Änderungen vorbehalten

to subject to unterziehen, unterwerfen;
vorbehaltlich

subject Fach

subliminal unterschwellig

to submit vorlegen, einreichen

subsequent anschließend, nachträglich

subsidiary Tochtergesellschaft

subsidies Subventionen

to subsist bestehen, existieren

to substantiate belegen

substitute Ersatz (durch etwas Ähnliches)

to sue and be sued klagen und verklagt werden

to suffer (er)leiden

to suit passen

suitable geeignet, passend

superb hervorragend

supervisory board Aufsichtsrat

supplier Lieferant, Zulieferer

to supply liefern

supply Angebot

to surge steil ansteigen, anschwellen

surname Familienname

surplus Überschuss

to surrender aushändigen, überlassen

survey report Schadensgutachten

survey Umfrage, Studie, Untersuchung

sympathy Beileid, Mitgefühl

t

table Tabelle

tailback Stau

tailor-made maßgeschneidert

to take a risk ein Risiko eingehen

to take account of berücksichtigen

to take advantage of in Anspruch nehmen

to take down aufschreiben, notieren

to take into account berücksichtigen

to take offence Anstoß nehmen

to take out insurance Versicherung abschließen

to take part teilnehmen

to take steps to Schritte unternehmen

to take the minutes Protokoll führen

to take turns sich abwechseln

to take up documents Dokumente entgegen-
nehmen

take-over Übernahme

target group Zielgruppe

target language Zielsprache

to target ins Visier nehmen, anpeilen,
ansteuern, anstreben, zielen auf

tariffs Zölle

task chair Arbeitsplatzstuhl

tax consultant Steuerberater(in)

tax refund Steuerrückerstattung

technically speaking genau genommen

tedious langweilig, lästig

temping agency Agentur für Zeitarbeit

template (Dokument)vorlage

temporarily vorübergehend

temporary vorübergehend, zeitweilig

to tend tendieren, dazu neigen

tentative vorsichtig

to terminate beenden

terms of business Geschäftsbedingungen

terms of payment and delivery Zahlungs- und Lieferbedingungen

territory Gebiet

the company in question das fragliche Unternehmen

the latter letztere(r/s)

the management die Geschäftsleitung

thereby dadurch

third-party insurance Haftpflichtversicherung

third-party Dritter, nicht beteiligte Partei

thistle Distel

those involved die Beteiligten

thought Gedanke

throughout überall (in)

thus so, somit

to tide over hinweghelfen über

tier of management Geschäftsleitungsebene, Managementebene

to tighten enger machen, verschärfen

time bill Nachsicht-, Zeit-, Zielwechsel, Wechsel mit Laufzeit

tiny contraption winzige Vorrichtung

to engrave (ein)gravieren

to hang on (colloquial) (warten)am Telefon (umgangssprachlich)

to the order of an die Order von

tool Werkzeug, Instrument

top priority höchste Priorität

torrential rain Platzregen

total amount Gesamtsumme

to total Gesamtsumme berechnen

(good) track record Erfolgsbilanz

trade discount Handelsrabatt, Wiederverkaufsrabatt

trade fair Fachmesse

trade journal Fachblatt, Fachzeitschrift

trade reference Geschäftsreferenz

trade terms Handelsbedingungen, -klauseln

trade visitors Fachbesucher

trade-off Kompromiss, Ausgleich

trainee Auszubildende(r), Trainee, Praktikant(in)

to transfer ownership Eigentumsrecht übertragen

transferable übertragbar

transmission Weiterleitung

travel agent Reisebüro

travel operator Reiseveranstalter

to treat behandeln

treatment Behandlung

treaty Vertrag (zwischen Staaten)

tremendous großartig, enorm

trial order Probeauftrag

tried and tested bewährt

trilateral dreiseitig

trough Tiefpunkt

to trust glauben, vertrauen, hoffen

trusted vertrauenswürdig

trusting vertrauensvoll

trustworthy vertrauenswürdig

tuber Pflanzenknolle

to tuck into hineinstecken

tumbler Becher, Trinkglas

turnover Umsatz

turn-taking Anstellen, Warten (bis man dran ist), Abwechseln

typewriter Schreibmaschine

u

umbrella organisation Dachverband

unaffordable unerschwinglich

unbusinesslike nicht geschäftsmäßig,-tüchtig

unconditional bedingungslos

unconditionally ohne Vorbehalt

to undercharge zu wenig berechnen

to underestimate unterschätzen

to undergo unterworfen sein

to underline unterstreichen

undertaking Verpflichtung

underwriter Versicherer, Versicherungsgeber

unfamiliar unbekannt, wenig vertraut

unfounded unbegründet

unified einheitlich, vereinigt

unique einzigartig

unit price Stückpreis

unlimited liability unbeschränkte Haftung

unloading Entladen

unreliable unzuverlässig

unsettled unbeständig, unruhig

unsolicited ungebeten, unverlangt

unsurpassed unübertroffen

unvalued policy Police ohne Wertangabe

upcoming bevorstehend, kommend

upholstered furniture Polstermöbel

upmarket gehoben, teuer, nobel

usage Gebrauch, Brauch

utensils Geräte, Instrumente

v

vacancy freie Stelle

to vacate (Hotelzimmer) räumen

valid gültig

validity Gültigkeit

value Wert

valued policy Police mit Wertangabe

variety Sorte, Vielfalt

various verschieden, unterschiedlich

VAT Mehrwertsteuer

vehicle Vehikel, Träger

vendor Verkäufer(in)

to ventilate belüften, lüften

venue Veranstaltungsort, Standort, Treffpunkt

verification Nach-, Überprüfung

vessel Schiff

via über

viable gangbar, praktikabel

vibrant lebhaft

vice versa umgekehrt

to view besichtigen

vintage Jahrgangs-(wein), klassisch

to violate verstoßen gegen

visible goods Waren, Güter

visitors' lounge Warteraum

volume buyer Großabnehmer

volume Umfang, Volumen, Menge

voting system Abstimmungsverfahren

voyage policy Einzelpolice

voyage Seereise, Seefahrt

w

war risk Kriegsrisiko

to warrant garantieren

warranty Garantie, Gewährleistung

water supply Wasserleitung

watershed Zeitgrenze

waybill Frachtbrief

we are anxious to uns liegt daran

we trust wir gehen davon aus

weapons Waffen, Kampfmittel

weight Gewicht

well-being Wohlergehen, Wohlbefinden

well-run gut geführt

were up by waren um ... gestiegen

wheat flour Weizenmehl

whereas während, wohingegen

whisky tumbler Whiskyglas

white goods Haushaltsgroßgeräte

whiteboard Weißwandtafel, Whiteboard

wholesaler Großhändler

wholly ganz, vollkommen

widely häufig, vielfach

widespread weit verbreitet

width Breite

willing bereit

willingness Bereitschaft

with effect from mit Wirkung von

with the utmost care mit äußerster Sorgfalt

with the utmost discretion mit äußerster
Diskretion

to withdraw money Geld abheben

to withhold zurückhalten

within a range of im Umkreis von

without engagement unverbindlich, frei-
bleibend

without fail mit Sicherheit, ganz bestimmt

without notice ohne (Vor-)Ankündigung

witness Zeuge, Zeugin

witty geistreich

woolly vage, unbestimmt

word by word Wort für Wort

working knowledge of Grundkenntnisse in

workload Arbeitsbelastung

workmanship Verarbeitung

woven gewebt

to wrap einschlagen, umhüllen

w

wristband heart-rate monitor Pulsuhr, Puls-
messgerät

y

to yield interest Zinsen abwerfen, sich
verzinsen

z

zip code Postleitzahl